THE WORLD ALMANAC®
BRAIN-BOOSTING
TRIVIA
CHALLENGES

THE WORLD ALMANAC®
BRAIN-BOOSTING
TRIVIA
CHALLENGES

150 LARGE-PRINT GAMES!

WORLD ALMANAC BOOKS

World Almanac books may be purchased in bulk at special discounts for sales promotion, corporate gifts, fundraising, or educational purposes. Special editions can also be created to specifications. For details, contact the Special Sales Department, 307 West 36th Street, 11th Floor, New York, NY 10018 or info@skyhorsepublishing.com.

Published by World Almanac Books, an imprint of Skyhorse Publishing, Inc., 307 West 36th Street, 11th Floor, New York, NY 10018.

The World Almanac® is a registered trademark of Skyhorse Publishing, Inc. All rights reserved.

www.skyhorsepublishing.com

10 9 8 7 6 5 4 3 2 1

Cover design by Melissa Gerber
Graphics by Shutterstock

Library of Congress Cataloging-in-Publication Data is available on file.

ISBN: 978-1-5107-7431-5

Printed in the United States of America

Pure Trivia

Animal Collectives

Match the group of animals with their associated collective nouns.

1. Coalition

2. Pod

3. Zeal

4. Smack

5. Congregation

6. Flamboyance

7. Parliament

8. Romp

9. Cackle

10. Charm

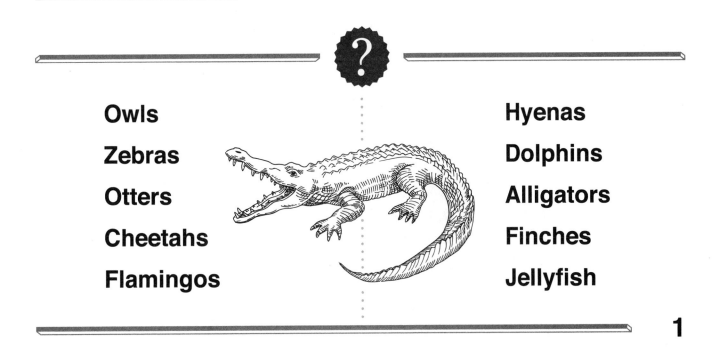

Owls

Zebras

Otters

Cheetahs

Flamingos

Hyenas

Dolphins

Alligators

Finches

Jellyfish

Pure Trivia

Do You Know Your U.S. National Parks?

See how many of these U.S. national parks you can recognize based on their well-known features! Double points if you can provide the states/territories they are located in.

1. This park is the world's first national park and has more than 10,000 geological thermal features.

2. Home to Mt. Whitney, this park also boasts the location of the world's largest tree.

3. This park sits on the Continental Divide of Colorado and has peaks of over 14,000 feet.

4. This park has more than 119 limestone caves and includes the Chihuahuan Desert.

5. This park is the largest remaining subtropical wilderness in the continental U.S.

6. Waters from this park's 47 hot springs are used for bathing and drinking.

7. This park is the location of a volcanic eruption that occurred about 7,700 years ago, and it is now the U.S.'s deepest lake.

8. This park is located on a peninsula that is also the highest elevation on the Eastern Seaboard.

9. This park is known for its beautiful beaches, Carib Indian petroglyphs, and evidence of colonial Danes.

10. Set in a scenic valley, this park features the country's highest waterfall, a grove of sequoias, and mountain faces that are popular for climbing.

11. Less than four hours from five other national parks and dozens of state parks, this park is the location of red rocks, vistas, and thousands of hoodoos.

Timed Test

Countries Beginning With the Letter S

Given 30 seconds, how many countries beginning with the letter S can you name?

_____   _____

_____   _____

_____   _____

_____   _____

_____   _____

_____   _____

_____   _____

_____   _____

_____   _____

_____   _____

Pure Trivia

Faces of U.S. Currency

Match all of the U.S. currency to the historical figures who appear on them.

1. Quarter

_____

2. Nickel

_____

3. $5 bill

_____

4. $20 bill

_____

5. $100 bill

_____

6. Half-dollar coin

7. $1 coin

_____

John F. Kennedy

Andrew Jackson

Benjamin Franklin

Sacagawea

Thomas Jefferson

George Washington

Abraham Lincoln

Alphabet Soup

Highest Rated Television Programs

Below are nine of the highest rated TV programs since 1951. In the mix, we have medical dramas, crime series, comedy sitcoms, and more. Do your best to unscramble the letters of each TV show.

1. I EVOL YUCL

_____

2. ZAANNOB

_____

3. EHT YADN RFFHTIIG WOHS

_____

4. YAPHP ASDY

_____

5. EFNSEDLI

_____

6. SFDRNIE

_____

7. EMCNAIRA LODI

_____

8. SNIC

_____

9. TEH IBG NAGB YTHROE

_____

Pure Trivia

Principal Wars of the U.S.

Arrange the list of wars in chronological order based on when they took place in history, starting with the earliest war and ending with the most recent.

1. _____

2. _____

3. _____

4. _____

5. _____

World War I

Vietnam War

Revolutionary War

Spanish-American War

Civil War

Pure Trivia

Major Wars in the World's History

This puzzle describes nine different wars that have been significant to the world's history. Match each description of events with the name of a war from the answer bank (keeping in mind that each description is but a minor piece of a very intricate and complicated whole).

1. This war was completed with the Battle of Hastings, a battle that took place on the English coast near Hastings, in which William I, duke of Normandy, defeated Harold II, Saxon king of England. The defeat led to the crowning of William in England, linking England's interests with those of the continent, and led to England's rise as a powerful monarchy.

2. Military expeditions undertaken by Western European Christians, usually at the behest of the papacy, to recover Jerusalem and other biblical places of pilgrimage from Muslim control.

3. Civil wars for the throne in England, fought by the rival houses of Lancaster and York. Richard, duke of York, clashed with King Henry VI of Lancaster and won. Richard died, and his son became King Edward IV.

4. A conflict between Great Britain and 13 British colonies on the North American continent.

5. In Europe, Germany and the Soviet Union attacked Poland, leading Britain and France to declare war on Germany, but Germany captured Paris. The U.S. entered the war. In the Pacific, Japan invaded China, joined forces with Germany and Italy, and signed a nonaggression pact with Russia.

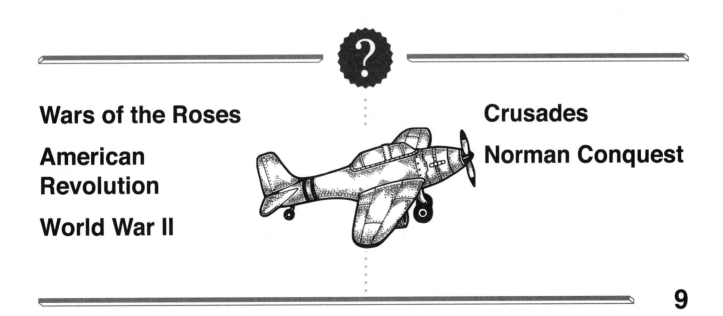

Wars of the Roses

American Revolution

World War II

Crusades

Norman Conquest

Pure Trivia

Early Egyptian Civilization

How well do you know the key players and symbols of the early Egyptians?

1. What was the plant used to make writing materials, as well as baskets, sandals, mats, ropes, tables, chairs, perfume, medicine, and more?

2. What is the name of the river that sustained life in Egypt?

3. What is the name of the large Egyptian structure depicting the mythical creature with the head of a human, the body of a lion, and the wings of a falcon?

4. What is the writing form that ancient Egyptians used?

5. Which famous Egyptian structures were built to honor and entomb ancient pharaohs?

Alphabet Soup

Top U.S. Franchises

While it's no surprise that some fast-food franchises are at the top, you may be surprised by some of the other companies that made *Entrepreneur* magazine's list of top franchises in the U.S. Use the clues below to unscramble the names.

1. Coffee, doughnuts, and baked goods
| UDNKNI

2. Tutoring and supplemental education
| NKUOM

3. Subs, Philly cheesesteaks | EYJERS SKEMI USBS

4. Fitness clubs | ANPLET FSINEST

5. Burgers, chicken, salads, and beverages
| SMDCLDONA

Pure Trivia

Names of Famous U.S. First Ladies

How well do you remember the names of the First Ladies? Use the answer bank to match first names to last names.

1. _____ Adams, wife of John Adams

2. _____ Roosevelt, wife of Franklin D. Roosevelt

3. _____ Rodham Clinton, wife of Bill Clinton

4. _____ Kennedy, wife of John F. Kennedy

5. _____ Washington, wife of George Washington

Hillary

Jacqueline

Martha

Abigail

Eleanor

Pure Trivia

Money-Making American Movies

How familiar are you with this century's most popular movies (so far)?

1. In the *Harry Potter* series, what is the name of Harry's godfather?

_____

2. Who are the six original Avengers?

_____

3. In *Lord of the Rings*, what are the names of the four hobbits who embark on the journey to defeat Sauron?

_____

4. In *Pirates of the Caribbean*, what is the nickname of young Will Turner's father?

_____

5. Which actor played the Joker in *The Dark Knight*?

_____

Picture This

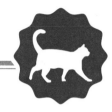

Popular Cat Breeds

Use the answer bank to label the pictures of popular cat breeds below.

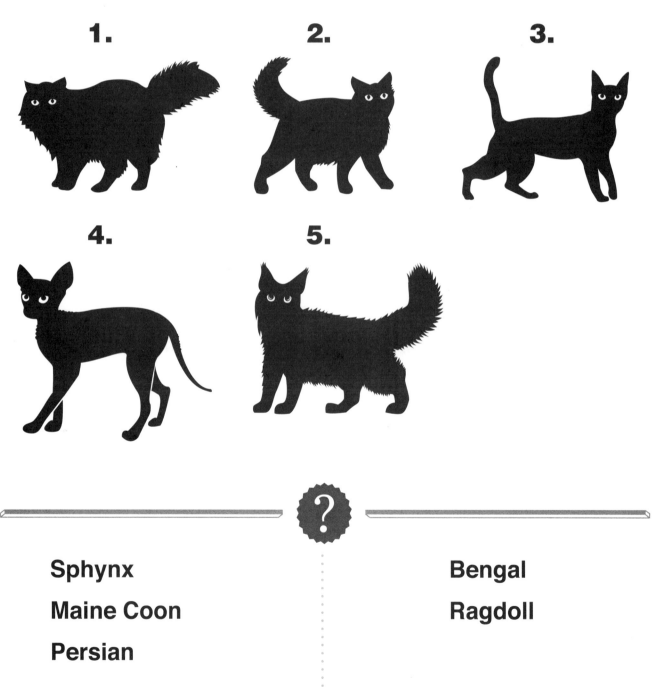

1.

2.

3.

4.

5.

Sphynx

Maine Coon

Persian

Bengal

Ragdoll

Timed Test

U.S. National Monuments

Given 30 seconds, how many of the U.S. National Parks Service's national monuments can you list? (Keep in mind that the National Parks Service distinguishes between National Monuments and National Memorials. For example, the Statue of Liberty is considered a National Monument; the Washington Monument is considered a National Memorial.)

Pure Trivia

The Scientific Revolution

Use the answer bank to label which scientist each breakthrough belonged to.

1. Promoted the heliocentric theory (the sun is at the center of the universe, not the Earth)

_____

2. Confirmed the heliocentric theory describing the elliptical orbits of the planets

_____

3. Formulated a model of the universe with the Sun at its center

_____

4. Best known for his laws of gravity and motion

_____

Isaac Newton

Nicolaus Copernicus

Johannes Kepler

Galileo Galilei

Alphabet Soup

Royal English Names

Of these five famous royal English names, each one should be familiar to you. Aside from being widely recognized from real figures in history lessons, these names have been included in lists of popular baby names for centuries. Test your recognition skills by unscrambling the five names below.

1. MIALWIL

4. ENAN

2. SARCLEH

5. ZHELIATBE

3. AJMES

Pure Trivia

Notable Writers of the Twentieth Century

Each written work below is—arguably—among its author's most famous works. Can you fill in each author's name? Keep in mind that the author may have been born in the nineteenth century but had their writing debut during the twentieth.

1. C _____ A _____ | *Things Fall Apart*

2. M _____ A _____ | *I Know Why the Caged Bird Sings*

3. E _____ C _____ | *The Very Hungry Caterpillar*

4. A _____ C _____ | *Murder on the Orient Express*

5. R _____ D _____ | *Charlie and the Chocolate Factory and Matilda*

Timed Test

Notable Ancient Greeks and Romans

Given 30 seconds, how many famous ancient Greek and Roman figures whose names begin with the letter *A* can you name? (Gods and goddesses from mythology are not included in the answers.)

Pure Trivia

Top-Grossing Classic American Movies

Match the movies with their descriptions.

1. An amusement park turns deadly

_____

2. A crime drama about a son's rise to power

_____

3. A historical romance set during the American Civil War

_____

4. An ungifted Alabama man has many memorable adventures

_____

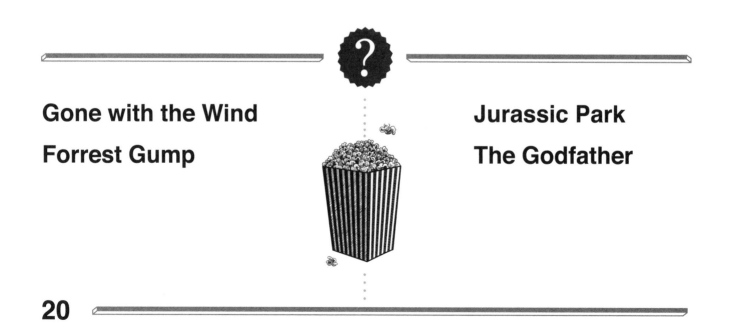

Gone with the Wind

Forrest Gump

Jurassic Park

The Godfather

Alphabet Soup

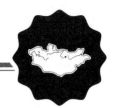

Mongolia

Most people know Mongolia for its deserts and nomadic tribes. Test how well you know Mongolia by unscrambling its various features, symbols, and history.

1. GSINGIN ANSDS

_____

2. ERD OHRE

_____

3. BIGO SERTDE

_____

4. OWSN RADEOLP

_____

5. EMALC

_____

Pure Trivia

Top Brands

All of the following brands are top brands, but which ones beat out the rest? In classic pop-quiz fashion, select the top brand for each of the products below.

1. Potato chips
   a. Wavy Lay's
   b. Lay's
   c. Ruffles
   d. Pringles

2. Salsa
   a. Tostitos
   b. Pace
   c. Herdez
   d. Chi-Chi's

3. Soft drinks
   a. Dr Pepper
   b. Mountain Dew
   c. Sprite
   d. Coca-Cola
   e. Pepsi

4. Toothpaste
   a. Sensodyne Pronamel
   b. Colgate Total
   c. Sensodyne
   d. Crest 3D White
   e. Colgate

5. Ice cream
   a. Häagen-Dazs
   b. Ben & Jerry's
   c. Blue Bell
   d. Breyers
   e. Edy's

Picture This

Visitors' Most Traveled-To Places in the U.S.

Visitors to the U.S. spend billions of dollars here every year. Which states do you think they travel to the most? Write in the names next to the images of each popular state.

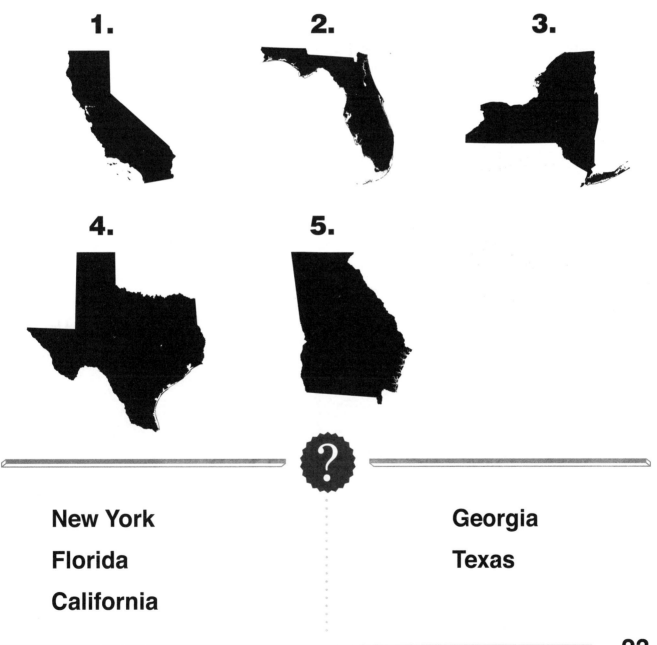

1.

2.

3.

4.

5.

New York

Florida

California

Georgia

Texas

Alphabet Soup

Corporations That Begin With the Letter *A*

Using the hints about the services each corporation provides, unscramble the following list to see 10 of the most well-known corporations whose names begin with the letter *A*.

1. Tech company founded by Steve Jobs
| LEPAP

2. Online retailer and e-commerce platform for products, video, music, books, and more
| NMAOZA

3. A financial institution that offers credit cards and travel-related services
| ICAAMNRE SPXRSEE

4. Grocery and drugstore
| NRSSOLBAET

5. Clothing and accessory company that focuses on athletic wear

SDADAI

6. Insurance for personal property and casualties

ELASLATT

7. An American-based airline company

KLSAAA RIA

8. Parent company of Google, YouTube, and Fitbit

AETAHBLP

9. Health insurance giant

NTAAE

10. Online booking service for vacation rentals

BBNIRA

Pure Trivia

Dietary Guidelines for Americans, 2020–2025

New U.S. government dietary guidelines are created every five years. According to the most recent guidelines, which nutrient-dense foods are encouraged? And which food groups should be limited?

Encouraged:

_____

_____

_____

_____

_____

Limited:

_____

_____

_____

_____

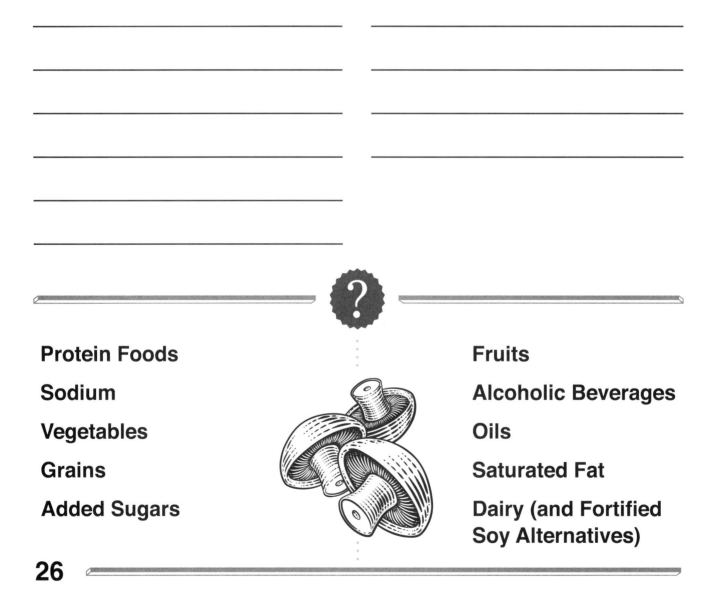

Protein Foods

Sodium

Vegetables

Grains

Added Sugars

Fruits

Alcoholic Beverages

Oils

Saturated Fat

Dairy (and Fortified Soy Alternatives)

Alphabet Soup

Most Crowded Countries

Unscramble the top five most densely populated countries.

1. ANOMOC

_____

2. PRINSAGEO

_____

3. TANVIAC YTCI

_____

4. HABIARN

_____

5. ALAMT

_____

Pure Trivia

Rock & Roll Hall of Famers

Do you know which Rock & Roll Hall of Famers wrote these classic hits? Fill in the blank with the name of the band or artist.

1. "Back in Black"

_____

2. "You Give Love a Bad Name"

_____

3. "I Don't Want to Miss a Thing"

_____

4. "Never Going Back Again"

_____

5. "Layla"

_____

Timed Test

Religions of the World

Given 30 seconds, how many major world religions can you think of? Check the answer key to see if you were able to hit all the major religions (and nonreligions) tracked in World Religion Database.

Pure Trivia

Animal Collectives

It doesn't sound that strange to our ears when we hear a group of hounds is called a *pack* or when we hear a group of ants is called a *colony*, but what about a *bale* of turtles or a *gaze* of raccoons? Match the animal collective noun with the animals given in the answer bank.

1. Convocation

_____

2. Bloat

_____

3. Smack

_____

4. Exaltation

_____

5. Mob

_____

6. Sleuth

_____

7. Obstinacy

_____

8. Siege

_____

9. Skulk

_____

10. Watch

_____

Bears

Jellyfish

Larks

Nightingales

Foxes

Buffalos

Kangaroos

Eagles

Cranes

Hippopotamuses

Pure Trivia

Common Acronyms

Do you know which phrases these common acronyms stand for?

1. AWOL

_____

2. BRB

_____

3. SCUBA

_____

4. MVP

_____

5. STEM

_____

Alphabet Soup

U.S. Constitution

Unscramble the words of this famous paragraph from the U.S. Constitution's Preamble.

"We the **OPELEP** _____ of the United States, in Order to form a more perfect **NIOUN** _____, establish **TECIJUS** _____, insure **CITOMDSE** _____ Tranquility, provide for the common **ECFDENE** _____, promote the general **ELWAFRE** _____, and secure the Blessings of **ILTYBRE** _____ to ourselves and our **ERSTOPYTI** _____, do ordain and **LSTAISHEB** _____ this **NOITUSTNOCTI** _____ for the United States of America."

Pure Trivia

Classical Composers

Match each composer with his musical piece(s).

1. *St. Matthew Passion* and *The Well-Tempered Clavier*

_____

2. *Moonlight Sonata, Emperor Concerto*, and 9 symphonies

_____

3. *The Four Seasons*

_____

4. *Nutcracker, Swan Lake*, and *The Sleeping Beauty*

_____

5. *Magic Flute, Marriage of Figaro*, and 41 symphonies

_____

Tchaikovsky

J.S. Bach

Mozart

Vivaldi

Beethoven

Picture This

Olympic Winter Sports

Label the images of the different sports below using the answer bank of sport names.

1.

2.

3.

4.

5.

Ice Hockey

Ski Jumping

Curling

Figure Skating

Snowboarding

Pure Trivia

U.S. Medals of Honor

In classic pop-quiz fashion, select the correct answer from each of the questions below.

1. What is the highest military award in the U.S. for individual bravery?
   a. Medal of Honor
   b. Distinguished Service Cross
   c. Silver Star
   d. Legion of Merit

2. What is the award that recognizes acts of heroism not involving actual conflict with an enemy?
   a. Medal of Honor
   b. Bronze Star
   c. Silver Star
   d. Soldier's Medal

3. What is the award for gallantry in action, performed with marked distinction?
   a. Legion of Merit
   b. Silver Star
   c. Air Medal
   d. Purple Heart

4. What is the award for single acts of heroism or meritorious achievement while participating in aerial flight?
   a. Army Commendation
   b. Air Medal
   c. Medal of Honor
   d. Purple Heart

Alphabet Soup

Top Sources of Sugar in U.S. Diets

Thanks to a national health survey from *Dietary Guidelines for Americans*, we have data about the main sources of sugar in U.S. diets. We bet you can guess the results too. Unscramble the words below to uncover the top five sugary items that Americans consume.

1. VERBESEGA

3. STARFBEAK ASCLEER

2. STERSEDS

4. ANYCD

Pure Trivia

Award-Winning Children's Books

Can you match each book's title to its description?

1. When Karana, a young girl, is left behind by her family and people, she must learn how to survive on her own.

2. A sci-fi novel about tesseract and the search for a father lost somewhere in time.

3. In Depression-era Michigan, a young boy's mother dies, and after four years of trying to survive on his own, he embarks on a journey to search for his father.

4. The Logan family fights to survive as a Black family in rural Mississippi during the Great Depression.

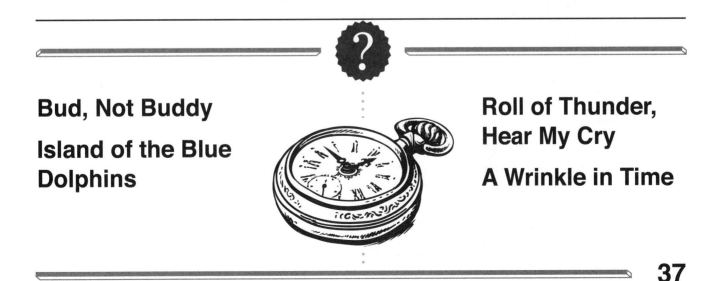

Bud, Not Buddy

Island of the Blue Dolphins

Roll of Thunder, Hear My Cry

A Wrinkle in Time

Pure Trivia

Components of Nutrition

How well do you know the little components that make up the food you consume every day? In classic pop-quiz fashion, select the correct answer from each of the questions below.

1. Which vitamin promotes good eyesight, helps with bone and cell growth, and supports your immune system?
   a. Vitamin K
   b. Niacin
   c. Iron
   d. Vitamin A

2. How can regular consumption of calcium help your body?
   a. Calcium supplies energy.
   b. Calcium builds and maintains bones and teeth.
   c. Calcium helps with red blood cell production.
   d. Calcium dissolves and transports nutrients.

3. All but one of the following are good sources of vitamin D. Which one is NOT a source of vitamin D?
   a. sunlight
   b. leafy vegetables
   c. fortified dairy products
   d. tuna

4. Which macronutrient helps build, maintain, and repair the body?
   a. Carbohydrates
   b. Fats
   c. Proteins
   d. Fiber

Timed Test

Countries Beginning With the Letter A

Given 30 seconds, how many countries beginning with the letter *A* can you name?

Pure Trivia

Notable Writers of the Twentieth Century

Each written work below is—arguably—among its author's most famous works. Can you fill in each author's name? Keep in mind that the author may have been born in the nineteenth century but had their writing debut during the twentieth.

1. F. S _____ F _____

| *The Great Gatsby*

2. R _____ F _____

| "Fire and Ice," "Nothing Gold Can Stay," and "The Road Not Taken"

3. W _____ G _____

| *Lord of the Flies*

4. E _____ H _____

| *The Old Man and the Sea*, *For Whom the Bell Tolls*, and *A Farewell to Arms*

5. J _____ J_____

| *Ulysses*, *Dubliners*, and *A Portrait of the Artist as a Young Man*

Pure Trivia

World's Wealthiest Individuals

Most of the world's wealthiest individuals have gained their wealth from being business owners. Use the businesses as clues to who some of the wealthiest Americans are. Initials have been provided to get you started.

1. Amazon | J _____ B_____

2. Microsoft | B _____ G_____

3. Berkshire Hathaway | W _____ B_____

4. Facebook/Meta | M _____ Z_____

5. Google/Alphabet | L _____ P_____

Pure Trivia

Things U.S. States Are Notable For

Use the clues below to see how much you know about different states in the U.S.

1. This state is known for its juicy peaches.

_____

2. This state is known for its red rocks.

_____

3. This state has the deepest lake in the nation.

_____

4. This state is known as the land of ten thousand lakes.

_____

5. This state is known for its large Mardi Gras festival, which it hosts every year.

_____

6. This state is known for its country music industry.

_____

7. This state is known for its nationally famous cheese.

_____

8. This state is home to the tallest building in the U.S.

_____

9. This state is the largest state in the U.S.

_____

10. This state is the smallest state in the U.S.

_____

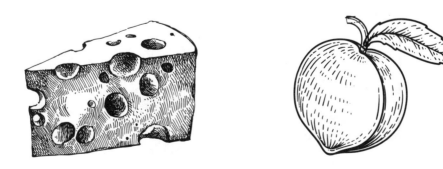

Pure Trivia

Top Motor Vehicle–Producing Nations

Determine the top five vehicle-producing nations based on the brands produced in those nations.

1. SAIC Motor

   Dongfeng

   FAW

   Chang'an _____

2. Ford

   Tesla

   Chevrolet

   Cadillac _____

3. Toyota

   Honda

   Nissan

   Mazda _____

4. Volkswagen

   Mercedes-Benz

   Audi

   BMW _____

5. Maruti Suzuki

   Tata

   Mahindra and Mahindra

   _____

Pure Trivia

Rock & Roll Hall of Famers

Do you know which Rock & Roll Hall of Famers wrote these classic hits? Fill in the blank with the name of the band or artist.

"Sweet Home Alabama"

_____

"Piano Man"

_____

"Edge of Seventeen"

_____

"Come Together"

_____

"Stairway to Heaven"

_____

Pure Trivia

Edison's Inventions

Thomas Edison held more than 1,000 patents. Can you match the descriptions of his inventions below with their names?

1. A motion-picture device for one viewer at a time

_____

2. A record player

_____

3. An early form of audio storage

_____

4. An electrical telegraph that could transmit and receive four signals at once

_____

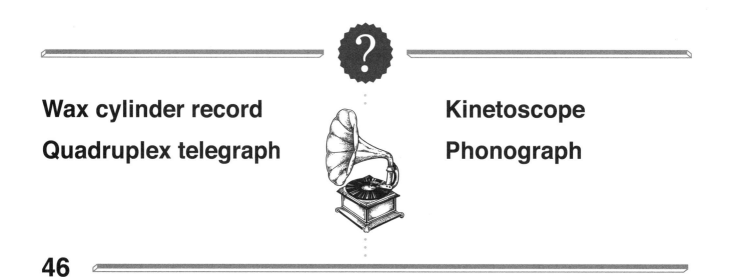

Wax cylinder record

Quadruplex telegraph

Kinetoscope

Phonograph

Pure Trivia

Innovation in Technology

Nowadays, people have a difficult time imagining what life would have been like without airplanes or without the internet at their fingertips and in their pockets. But it wasn't that long ago that some of our most commonly used technologies were just budding ideas. See if you can put each form of technology below into chronological order of invention by numbering the entries. Bonus points if you know the years!

_____ The Wright Brothers invent the first motor-powered airplane

_____ Invention of the first smartphone

_____ Apple releases the first iPhone

_____ Gutenberg brings movable type to Europe

_____ The first successful permanent transatlantic telegraph cable is laid

Alphabet Soup

Test Your Knowledge of the Last Frontier

Most people know Alaska for its cold expanse, long daylight hours, and great national parks. Test how well you know Alaska by unscrambling its various features and symbols below.

1. HERNTRON GHITLS

2. GINSFIH

3. IDNMITGH NSU

4. EUJAUN

5. OGD GMUNSIH

Pure Trivia

U.S. Capitals

Fill in the blanks next to the state capitals with their respective states.

1. Springfield _____

2. Sacramento _____

3. Tallahassee _____

4. Boise _____

5. Bismarck _____

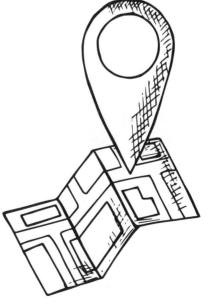

Pure Trivia

Award-Winning Children's Books

The Newbery Medal is awarded annually to the most distinguished contributions to American children's literature. Some of these stories are deeply engraved in the memories of our own childhood or of reading to children and grandchildren. Can you match each book's title to its author?

1. Maniac Magee

4. Walk Two Moons

2. Holes

5. The Tale of Despereaux

3. The Giver

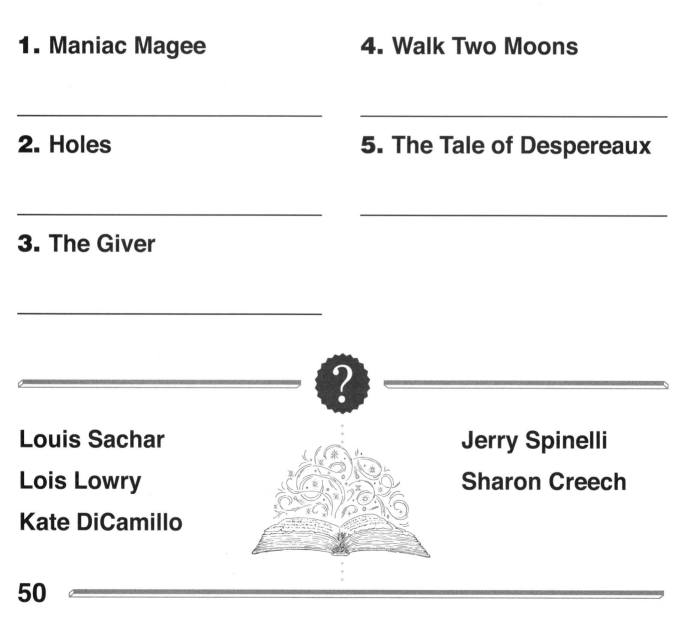

Louis Sachar

Jerry Spinelli

Lois Lowry

Sharon Creech

Kate DiCamillo

Picture This

Baby Animals

Who doesn't love baby animals? Use the answer bank of baby animal names to label the pictures below.

1.

2.

3.

4.

5.

?

Gosling

Hoglet

Cygnet

Joey

Lamb

Pure Trivia

Notable Writers of the Twentieth Century

Each written work below is—arguably—among its author's most famous works. Can you fill in each author's name? Keep in mind that the author may have been born in the nineteenth century but had their author debut during the twentieth.

1. G _____ O _____

Animal Farm and *Nineteen Eighty-Four*

2. J. D. S _____

The Catcher in the Rye

3. D _____. S_____

The Cat in the Hat

4. J _____ S _____

The Grapes of Wrath and *Of Mice and Men*

5. J. _____. T_____

The Hobbit and *The Lord of the Rings*

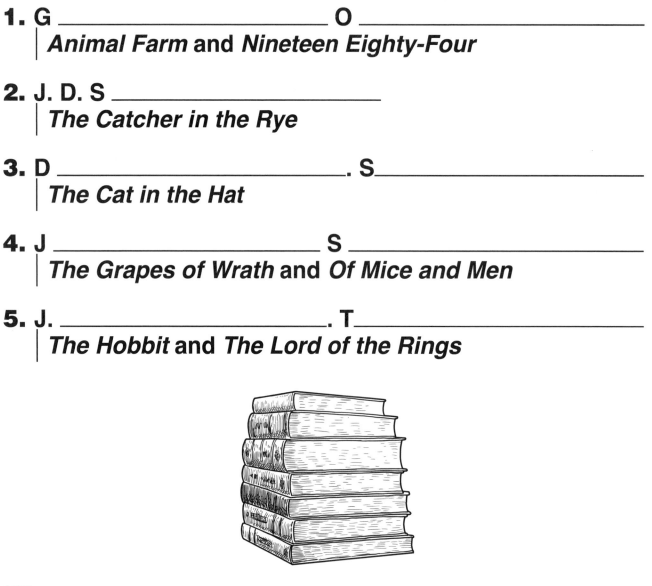

Alphabet Soup

Early Christian Art and Design

Use the images below to unscramble the names of some features and symbols of early Christian art and design.

1. TORUSUORDBA

2. CGITOH

3. NESMORAUEQ

4. DEAINST SLASG

5. FRELEI SERUTCPLU

Pure Trivia

Origins of the Names of U.S. States

Match each etymology (name origin) with its state name.

1. From the Spanish word for "colored red," which was originally given to the state's most significant river

_____

2. From the Aztec word for "silver-bearing"

_____

3. From Apache and Pueblo words meaning "those who are higher up," in reference to a tribe living in the area

_____

4. From the Chippewa phrase *mici gama*, meaning "great water"

_____

5. From the French words for "green" and "mountain"

_____

Michigan

Utah

Vermont

Colorado

Arizona

Pure Trivia

Common Abbreviations

Do you know which words these common abbreviations are short for?

1. tsp

_____

2. yuppie

_____

3. etc.

_____

4. c.

_____

5. Sgt.

_____

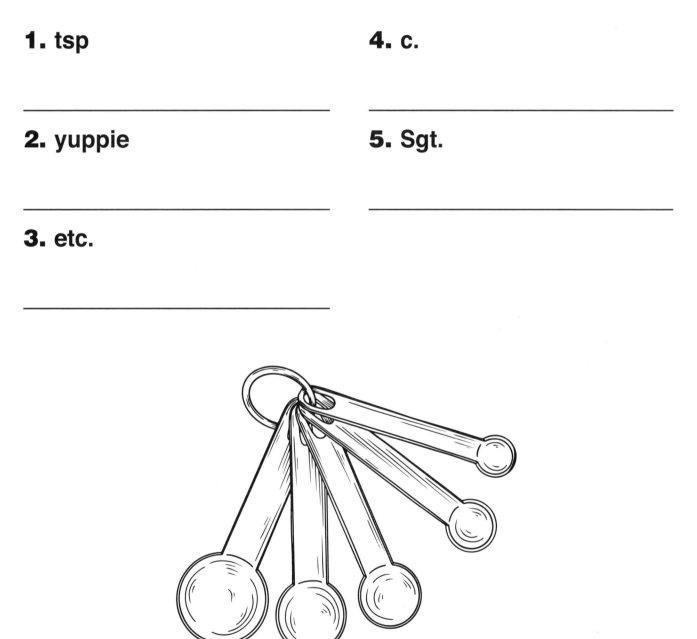

Timed Test

Countries Beginning With the Letter *B*

Given 30 seconds, how many countries beginning with the letter *B* can you name?

Pure Trivia

U.S. Capitals

Fill in the blanks next to the state capitals with their respective states.

1. Hartford _____

2. Augusta _____

3. Boston _____

4. Jackson _____

5. Helena _____

Pure Trivia

Timeline of Architectural Styles

The timeline of architectural styles below shows the approximate years when the styles surfaced in history. The timeline is missing some of history's essential periods. Using the answer bank, fill in the missing styles on the timeline.

Mesopotamian c. 3500 BCE

1. _____ **c. 3000** BCE

Minoan c. 1800 BCE

Greek c. 750 BCE

2. _____ **c. 500** BCE

Qin and Han c. 221 BCE

Sui and Tang 581 CE

Romanesque c. 900

Gothic c. 1100

3. _____ **c. 1420**

Mughal 1526

Neoclassicism 1750

Art Nouveau 1884

4. _____ **1925**

5. _____ **1970**

Art Deco

Postmodernism

Renaissance

Egyptian

Roman

Alphabet Soup

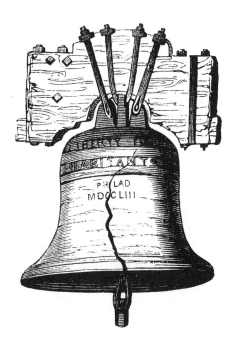

U.S. Declaration of Independence

Use the answer bank to unscramble the words of this famous paragraph from the Declaration of Independence.

"We hold these **THUSRT** _____ to be self-

TEVDNEI _____, that all **NME** _____

are created **LQAEU** _____, that they are

endowed by their **ATCRERO** _____ with certain

unalienable **GRHITS** _____, that among these

are **ELFI** _____, **RYTLBIE** _____,

and the **TIUPSRU** _____ of **PIHNEPSAS**

_____

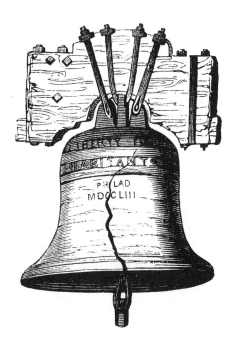

Pure Trivia

Grammy Awards

Match each artist with their Grammy Award–winning record of the year.

1. "Moon River"

_____

2. "Mrs. Robinson"

_____

3. "Hotel California"

_____

4. "Just the Way You Are"

_____

5. "It's Too Late"

_____

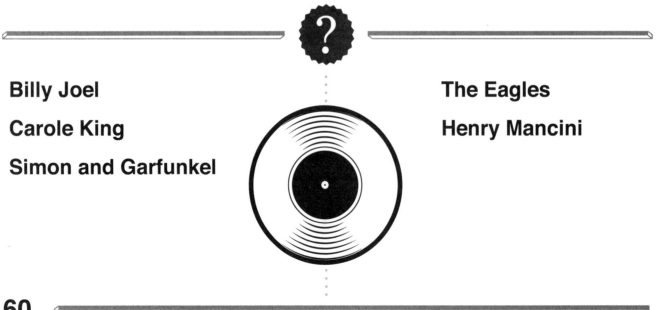

Billy Joel

Carole King

Simon and Garfunkel

The Eagles

Henry Mancini

Picture This

Life Cycles of Animals

See if you can identify the five animals below by their pictures. Then, order the animals from shortest average life span to longest average life span.

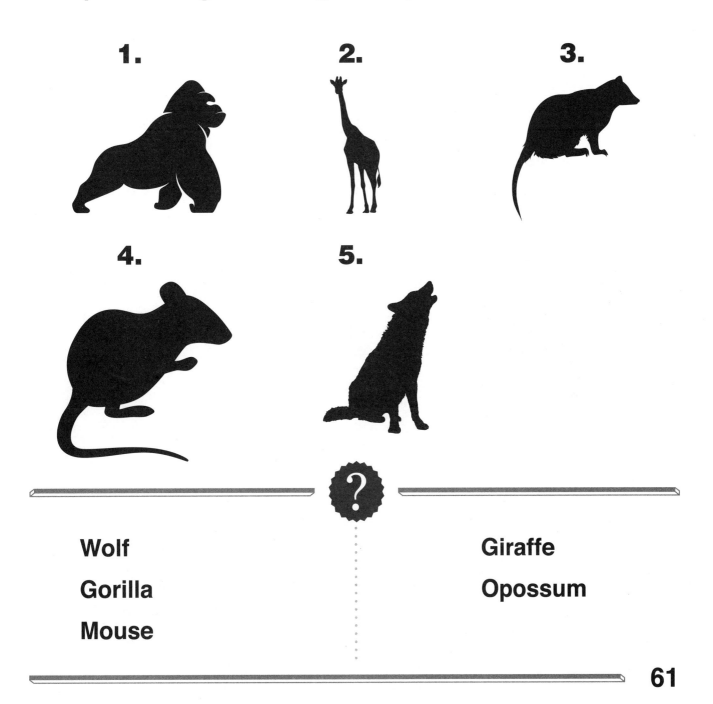

1.

2.

3.

4.

5.

Wolf

Gorilla

Mouse

Giraffe

Opossum

Picture This

Olympic Summer Sports

Label the images of the different sports below using the answer bank of sport names.

1.

2.

3.

4.

5.

Tennis

Volleyball

Track & Field

Swimming & Diving

Gymnastics

Pure Trivia

Academy Awards (Oscars) for Best Picture

Fill in the blanks in the chart below using the names of movies and the actors or actresses who performed in them. Note that while all films here were best picture winners, not all of the actors and actresses in them were winners—or even nominated!

Picture	Actor	Actress
A	Clark Gable	Vivien Leigh
Casablanca	**B**	Ingrid Bergman
My Fair Lady	Rex Harrison	**C**
The Sound of Music	Christopher Plummer	**D**
One Flew Over the Cuckoo's Nest	**E**	Louise Fletcher
F	Marlon Brando & Al Pacino	Talia Shire & Diane Keaton
G	Dustin Hoffman & Tom Cruise	Valeria Golino
The Silence of the Lambs	Anthony Hopkins	**H**
Schindler's List	**I**	Embeth Davidtz
J	Mel Gibson	Sophie Marceau

Pure Trivia

English's Borrowed Words and Phrases

Match the following list of English's borrowed words and phrases with their definitions. Bonus points if you can say whether the word or phrase is borrowed from Latin, Greek, French, German, Yiddish, Swedish, or Tamil.

1. impromptu; for the end or purpose at hand

_____

_____

2. audacity or nerve

_____

_____

3. a double or counterpart of a person

_____

_____

4. a person or event that provides an unexpected, often miraculous and contrived, solution to a problem

_____

_____

5. "I don't know what"; the little something that eludes description

_____

_____

6. a person who receives, investigates, and settles complaints

_____

_____

7. an outcast; a member of a lower class or caste

_____

_____

8. an unwelcome person

_____

_____

9. the masses

_____

_____

je ne sais quoi

persona non grata

doppelganger

ombudsman

chutzpa

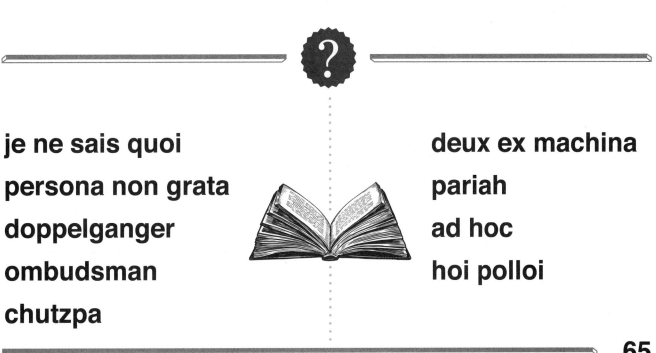

deux ex machina

pariah

ad hoc

hoi polloi

Pure Trivia

Basic First Aid

Match the answers in the bank of injuries and emergencies to the first aid assistance that is recommended.

1. Cover the wound with a sterile dressing and apply direct pressure to stop the flow. Cover compress with a bandage and call 911 if flow is severe.

2. Call 911 immediately. Do not move the person if a spinal injury is suspected.

3. Call 911. After obtaining permission (if person is conscious) deliver five blows to the back followed by five thrusts to the abdomen.

Choking   Unconsciousness

Bleeding

Alphabet Soup

Test Your Knowledge of the Wolverine State

Most people know Michigan for its stunning shorelines, innovative automobile industry, and great fishing. Test how well you know Michigan by unscrambling its various features and symbols below.

1. CAMIKANC INDSLA

4. TEIWH NPEI

2. OTIRTDE

5. NTGMAFUCRIANU

3. ROTMO IYCT

Pure Trivia

Notable Writers of the Nineteenth Century

Each written work below is—arguably—among its author's most famous works. Can you fill in each author's name? Keep in mind that the author may have been born in the eighteenth century but had their writing debut during the nineteenth.

1. L _____ M _____

A _____ | *Little Women*

2. J _____ A _____

| *Pride and Prejudice, Emma*, and *Sense and Sensibility*

3. E _____ B _____

| *Wuthering Heights*

4. L _____ C _____

| *Alice's Adventures in Wonderland*

5. C _____ D _____

| *Great Expectations, Oliver Twist*, and *A Tale of Two Cities*

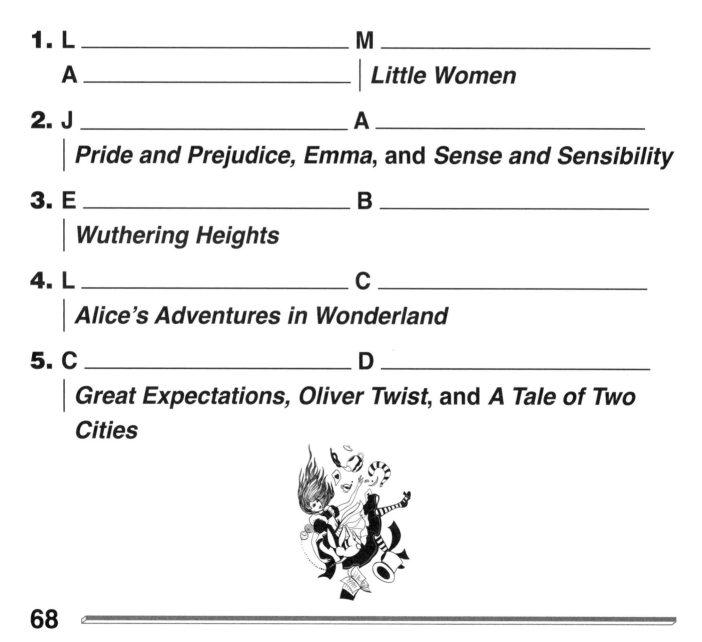

Pure Trivia

Puzzling Pseudonyms

For one reason or another, many entertainers choose to use a pseudonym or stage name. Most entertainers brand their stage names so well that the public never knows their real name. See if you can guess the true identities of some of these famous entertainers by matching the entertainer names with their less-famous counterparts.

1. Eleanora Fagan

4. Anna Mae Bullock

2. Norma Jeane Mortenson (Baker)

5. Reginald Dwight

3. Virginia McMath

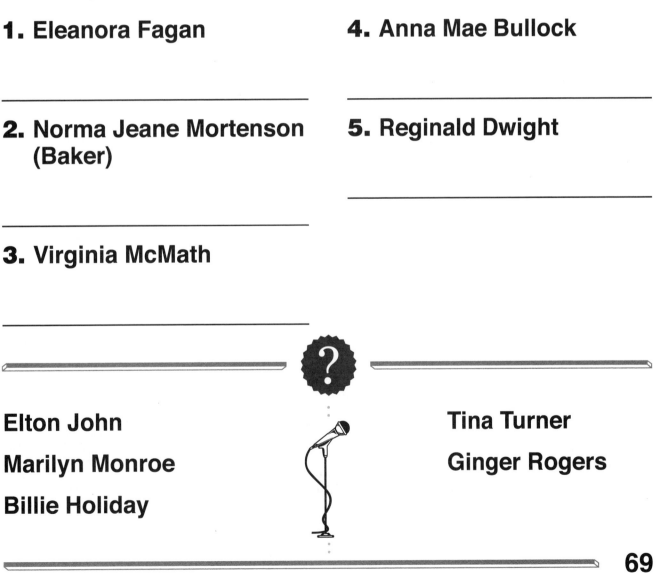

Elton John

Marilyn Monroe

Billie Holiday

Tina Turner

Ginger Rogers

Timed Test

G

Countries Beginning With the Letter *G*

Given 30 seconds, how many countries beginning with the letter *G* can you name?

_____   _____

_____   _____

_____   _____

_____   _____

_____   _____

_____   _____

_____   _____

_____   _____

_____   _____

_____   _____

Pure Trivia

Mohs Scale of Hardness

In 1812, German mineralogist Friedrich Mohs created a scale to measure the relative hardness of 10 different minerals. These minerals are numbered 1 to 10, with 10 being the hardest mineral, meaning that it is the most scratch resistant. Below, you've been given number 1 and number 10 on the scale. Fill in numbers 2–9 using the answer bank

1. Talc (the **softest**, **least** scratch-resistant mineral)

2. _____

3. _____

4. _____

5. _____

6. _____

7. _____

8. _____

9. _____

10. Diamond (the **hardest**, **most** scratch-resistant mineral)

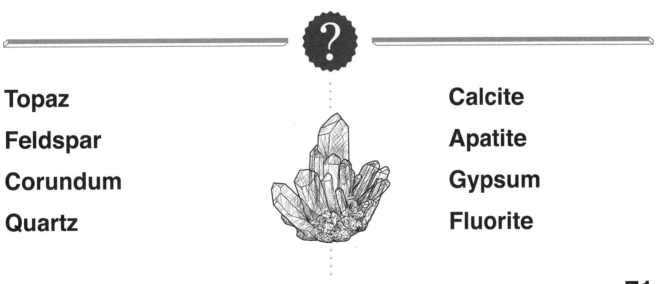

Topaz

Feldspar

Corundum

Quartz

Calcite

Apatite

Gypsum

Fluorite

Alphabet Soup

Top Sources of Saturated Fat in U.S. Diets

The results are in! Thanks to a national health survey from *Dietary Guidelines for Americans*, we have data about the main sources of saturated fat in U.S. diets. We bet you can guess the results too. Unscramble the words below to uncover the top five items containing saturated fat that Americans consume.

1. CHEISDNSAW

_____

2. ESRTSDES

_____

3. CERI/ASTPA HISSED

_____

4. KIML

_____

5. ZAPZI

_____

Pure Trivia

Most Populated U.S. Cities

In which states are the following most populated cities?

1. New York

4. Philadelphia

_____

2. Los Angeles

5. Dallas

_____

3. Chicago

_____

Pure Trivia

Notable Writers of the Nineteenth Century

Each written work below is—arguably—among its author's most famous works. Can you fill in each author's name? Keep in mind that the author may have been born in the eighteenth century but had their writing debut during the nineteenth.

1. A _____ D _____

   The Count of Monte Cristo and *The Three Musketeers*

2. R _____ W _____

   E _____ "Nature," "The Over-Soul,"

   and "Self-Reliance"

3. N _____ H _____

   The Scarlet Letter

4. V _____ H _____

   Les Misérables

5. J _____ K _____

   "Ode to a Nightingale" and "Ode on a Grecian Urn"

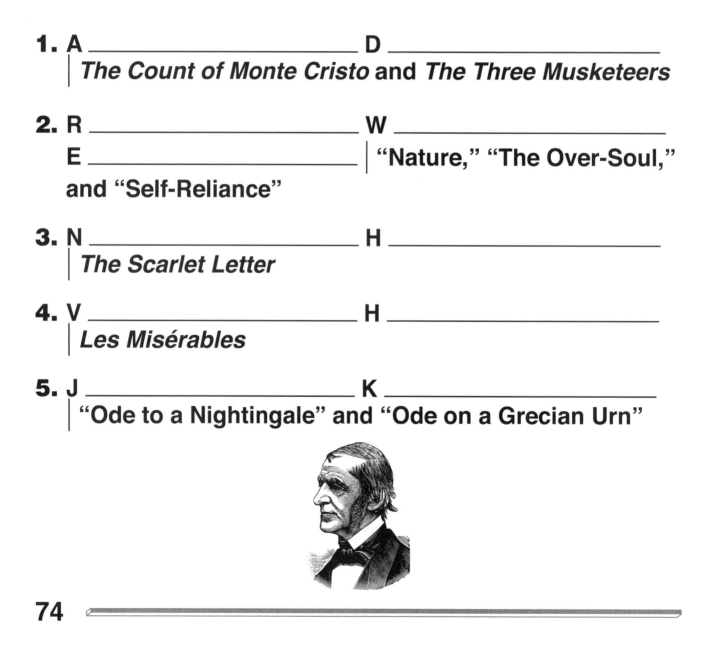

Pure Trivia

The Bill of Rights—10 Amendments

Label the number of each Amendment found in the Bill of Rights based on their descriptions.

1. _____: Prohibits cruel and unusual punishments

2. _____: Protects freedom of speech and religion

3. _____: Protects freedom to keep and bear arms

4. _____: Protects the right to a public and speedy trial in criminal cases

5. _____: Powers not given to the federal government are given to the independent states

6. _____: Assures recognition of additional rights that people have but are not covered in the Bill of Rights

7. _____: Prohibits arrests without warrants and unreasonable searches and seizures

8. _____: Prohibits being forced to quarter soldiers

9. _____: Ensures due process, protects against forced self-incrimination, and prohibits being tried for the same crime twice

10. _____: Protects the right to a trial by jury

Alphabet Soup

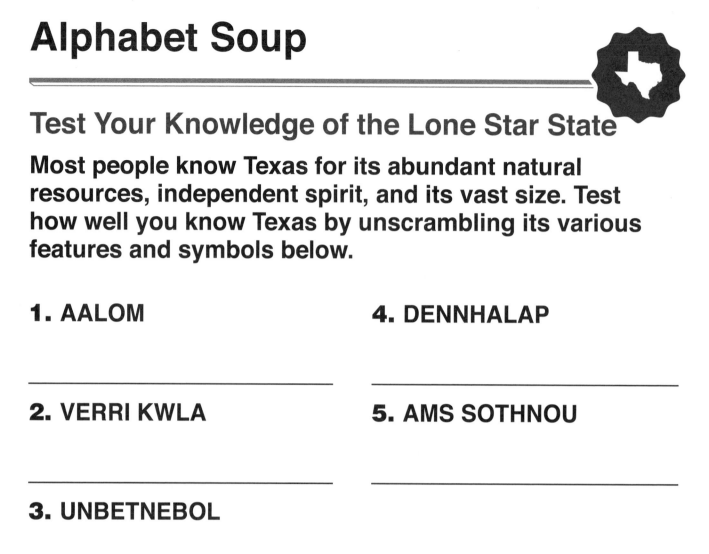

Test Your Knowledge of the Lone Star State

Most people know Texas for its abundant natural resources, independent spirit, and its vast size. Test how well you know Texas by unscrambling its various features and symbols below.

1. AALOM

2. VERRI KWLA

3. UNBETNEBOL

4. DENNHALAP

5. AMS SOTHNOU

Pure Trivia

Modern History: 1997

It was the year of *Buffy the Vampire Slayer* and the Spice Girls. See what else you remember from 1997.

1. Which NASA mission landed on the surface of Mars on July 4, 1997?

2. Which beloved royal passed away from a Paris car crash on August 31, 1997? Hint: An estimated 2.5 billion people viewed her funeral.

3. Which James Cameron blockbuster starring Leonardo DiCaprio and Kate Winslet went on to win 11 Oscars and take the title of top-grossing film of all time?

4. The first novel of which popular series was published in the UK by Bloomsbury in 1997? Hint: This series of seven fantasy novels follows a young wizard.

5. Which Celine Dion hit single served as the major theme song for the blockbuster mentioned above?

Timed Test

Great Impressionists

Given 30 seconds, how many well-known Impressionist artists of the nineteenth century can you list?

Pure Trivia

New English Words

Using the answer bank, match these relatively new dictionary entries with their definitions.

1. Compromising information that is used to blackmail or discredit a person or group, usually for political purposes

2. Health care provided remotely to a patient in a separate location

3. Overly optimistic and unrealistic thinking about the future

4. Location information added to a digital file or image

Kompromat

Geotag

Telehealth

Blue Sky

Pure Trivia

Early Notable Writers

Each written work below is—arguably—among its author's most famous works. Can you fill in each author's name?

1. G _____ C _____
   The Canterbury Tales

2. M _____ de C _____
   Saavedra | *Don Quixote*

3. D _____ A _____
   The Divine Comedy

4. J _____ M _____
   Paradise Lost

5. W _____ S _____
   Romeo and Juliet, King Lear, Hamlet, and more

Alphabet Soup

Who Owns What?

How well do you know the U.S. parent companies of these well-known consumer brands? Each of the brand groupings below has a parent company. Unscramble the accompanying names of the parent companies.

1. Pepperidge Farm, Prego, V8 | BEPLMACL UPOS

2. Dreyer's, Gerber, Hot Pockets, Perrier, Purina | ÉSTLEN

3. Brita, Glad, Hidden Valley, Kingsford, Pine-Sol | ORXLOC

4. Aquafina, Doritos, Frito-Lay's, Gatorade, Mountain Dew, Quaker Oats, Rice-A-Roni, Tropicana | PCOPSIE

5. Band-Aid, Benadryl, Listerine, Neosporin, Neutrogena, Rogaine, Tylenol, Visine | OHSNJNO & NOSHNJO

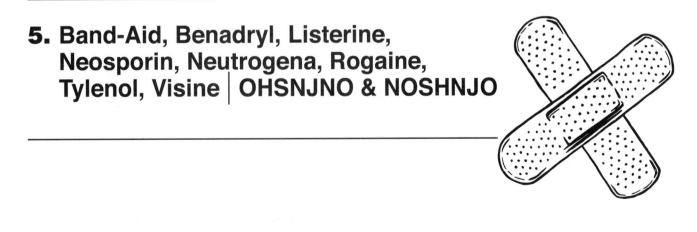

Picture This

Famous Historical Architecture

Give the silhouettes of famous architecture their proper names. Bonus points if you can provide their location. One has already been done for you.

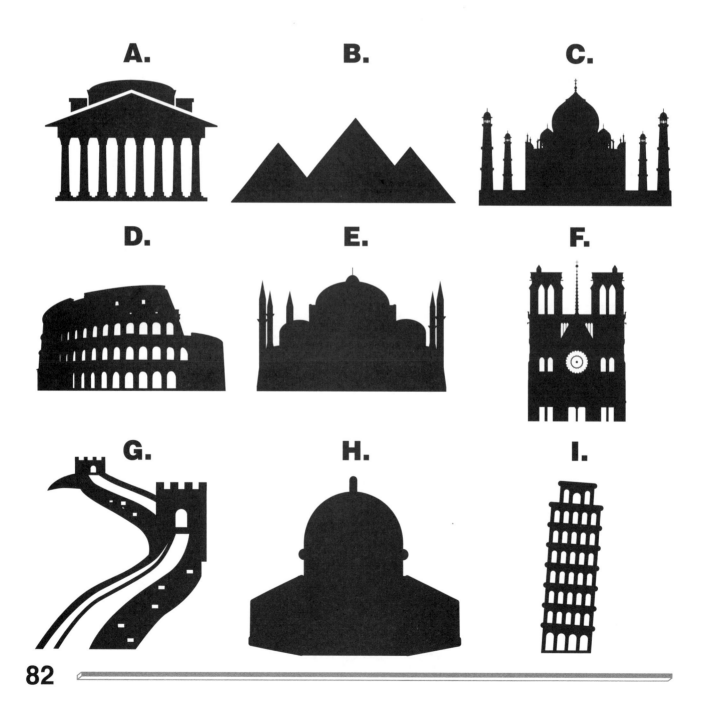

A.

B.

C.

D.

E.

F.

G.

H.

I.

1. Taj Mahal

C

India

2. Dome of the Rock

3. Pantheon

4. Colosseum

5. Great Wall

6. Leaning Tower of Pisa

7. Cathedral of Notre Dame

8. Hagia Sophia

9. Pyramids of Giza

Alphabet Soup

Space Missions

There have been dozens of notable lunar and planetary science missions, each given a special name. Use the clues about the missions' launch dates and purposes to unscramble the names.

1. 2004: provided images of Mercury before eventually landing on its surface | GERSENMES

2. 1989: while on its way to Jupiter, made a flyby of Venus; assisted in the study of Jupiter and its moons | AGEOLIL

3. 1989: mapped about 98 percent of Venus's surface, showing that at least 85 percent is volcanic | GELNALAM

4. 1977: encountered Jupiter, Saturn, Uranus, and Neptune; confirmed existence of Neptune's rings | AREGYVO 2

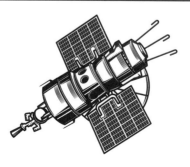

Timed Test

Venomous Animals

Given 30 seconds, how many venomous animals can you think of?

_____   _____

_____   _____

_____   _____

_____   _____

_____   _____

_____   _____

_____   _____

_____   _____

_____   _____

_____

Picture This

World's Speediest Species

Use the pictures below to figure out five of the world's speediest runners.

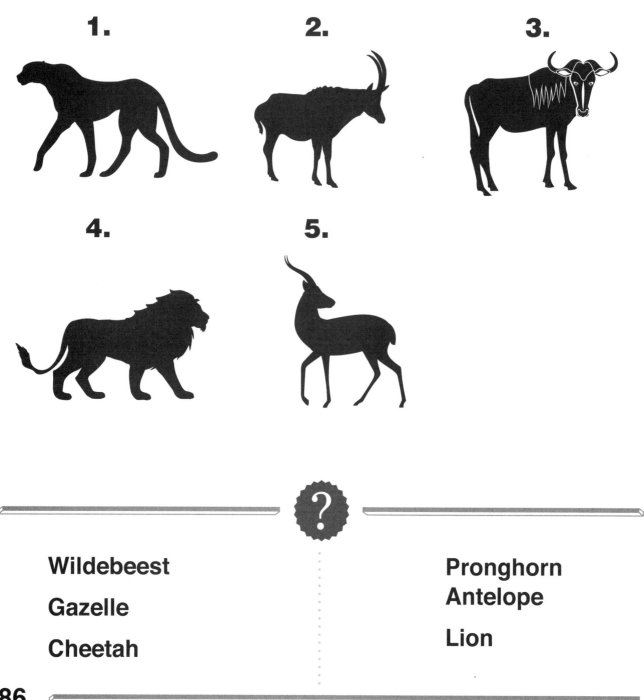

1.

2.

3.

4.

5.

?

Wildebeest

Gazelle

Cheetah

Pronghorn Antelope

Lion

Alphabet Soup

Corporations That Begin With the Letter *B*

Using the hints about the services each corporation provides, unscramble the following list to see 5 of the most well-known corporations whose names begin with the letter *B*.

1. Bookseller and publisher | SNEBRA & BLEON

2. Realty company; also, the parent company of GEICO, Fruit of the Loom, Dairy Queen, and Duracell | RIEKBHERS ATHAHYWA

3. Retailer for software, appliances, and electronics | SBTE YBU

4. Manufacturer of commercial jets and military aircrafts | IGEBON

5. Banking and financial services | KBNA FO MAACRIE

Pure Trivia

Animal Collectives

It doesn't sound that strange to our ears when we hear a group of hounds is called a *pack* or when we hear a group of ants is called a *colony*, but what about a *parliament* of owls or a *gaze* of raccoons? Match the animal collective noun with the animals given in the answer bank.

1. Raft

_____

2. Cloud

_____

3. Leap

_____

4. Muster

_____

5. Bale

_____

6. Intrusion

_____

7. Unkindness

_____

8. Bevy

_____

9. Kaleidoscope

_____

10. Clowder

_____

Ravens
Peacocks
Turtles
Butterflies
Swans

Cockroaches
Cats
Ducks
Leopards
Locusts

Picture This

Famous Landmarks in the City of Lights

Use the answer bank to label the images of Paris landmarks.

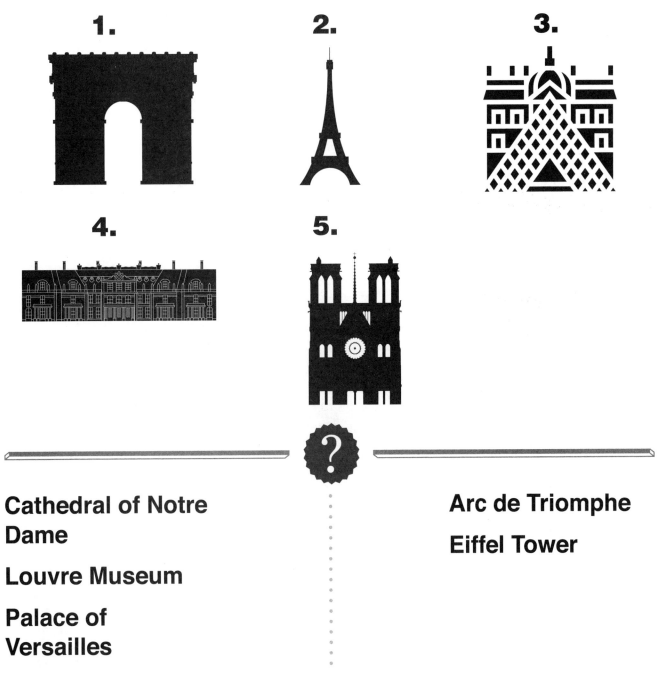

1.

2.

3.

4.

5.

Cathedral of Notre Dame

Louvre Museum

Palace of Versailles

Arc de Triomphe

Eiffel Tower

Alphabet Soup

Major U.S. Airlines

Unscramble the names of 5 major U.S. airlines.

1. STEWTOHUS

_____

2. MCAINRAE

_____

3. TELDA

_____

4. IDUTEN

_____

5. UBJELTE

_____

Timed Test

Ages of Earth's History

Given 30 seconds, how many of Earth's eons, eras, periods, and epochs can you list?

_____   _____

_____   _____

_____   _____

_____   _____

_____   _____

_____   _____

_____   _____

_____   _____

_____   _____

_____   _____

_____   _____

Pure Trivia

Modern History: 1972

It's hard to believe that more than 50 years have passed since the release of Stevie Wonder's "Superstition" and the publication of Roger Kahn's *The Boys of Summer*. See what else you can remember from that year.

1. What is the name given to the date January 30, 1972, when British forces fatally shot 13 unarmed protesters in Derry, Northern Ireland?

2. After approval by the U.S. Senate on March 22, 1972, which amendment banning discrimination on the basis of sex was sent to the states for ratification?

3. Five men were arrested on June 17, 1972, for breaking into the Democratic National Committee offices in Washington, DC. What is the name of the hotel-and-office complex that gave the name to the resulting political scandal?

4. What was the name of NASA's sixth and final mission in which humans set foot on the moon?

Alphabet Soup

Tony Award–Winning Musicals

Unscramble the names of five award-winning musicals.

1. ESL LSAÉMEIRSB

_____

2. HMOPATN FO HTE ERPOA

_____

3. TEH USODN FO CSUMI

_____

4. DRELFID NO EHT OROF

_____

5. STCA

_____

Pure Trivia

Baby Animals

Who doesn't love baby animals? Match the official terms for the newborns of a species to the correct animals.

1. Goat

_____

2. Frog

_____

3. Seal

_____

4. Pigeon

_____

5. Jellyfish

_____

Squab

Pup

Ephyra

Kid

Tadpole

Alphabet Soup

Royal Scottish Names

While the names of historical Scottish royalty perhaps aren't as common today in the U.S. as their English counterparts, some of these Scottish names have certainly come back into style in recent years. Test your recognition skills by unscrambling the five names below.

1. TORERB

4. YAMR

2. ASJEM

5. RGTEARMA

3. NAEXRADEL

Timed Test

Baseball's American League

Given 30 seconds, how many of the teams in Major League Baseball's American League can you list? Check the answer key to see whether you got all 15.

Alphabet Soup

Top-Selling Light Trucks in the U.S.

Unscramble the names of these top-selling light trucks to see the highest-ranking models sold in 2021.

1. DFRO F-ESRISE

2. MRA UPCIPK

3. ELTOVRHEC DISOLAERV

4. OYTAOT V4RA

5. DHANO C-VR

Picture This

Best-in-Show Dog Breeds

It's hard to resist cute dogs, but well-behaved, perfectly groomed dogs? That takes the cake—or the best-in-show award. Choose from the bank of best-in-show dog breeds to label the pictures of the pups below.

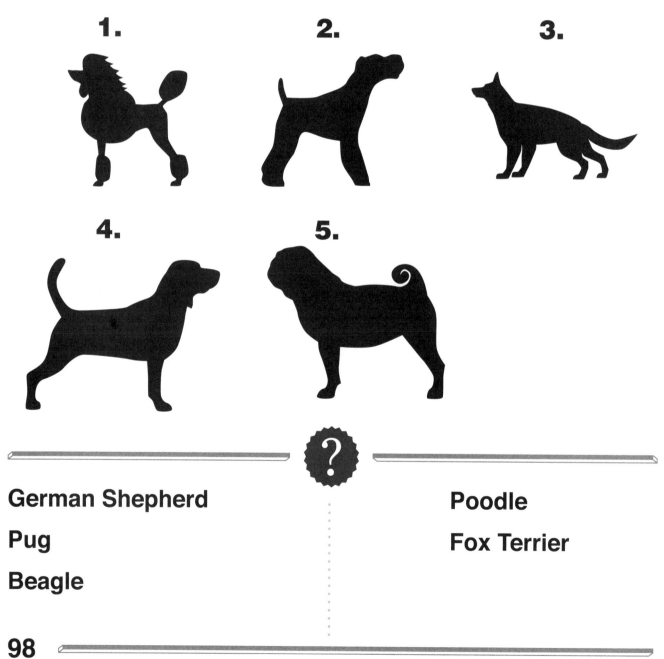

1.

2.

3.

4.

5.

German Shepherd

Pug

Beagle

Poodle

Fox Terrier

Alphabet Soup

Countries With Deserts

This is a list of well-known deserts. Unscramble the letters to determine in which countries the deserts are located.

1. Mojave Desert
NITUNDE ETSATS

2. Nubian Desert | DUSNA

3. Patagonian Desert
TGANRAIE

4. Great Victoria Desert
UASLATIRA

5. Sinai Desert | YPGET

Timed Test

B

Country Capitals Beginning With the Letter *B*

Give yourself 30 seconds to list country capital cities that begin with the letter *B*.

_____   _____

_____   _____

_____   _____

_____   _____

_____   _____

_____   _____

_____   _____

_____   _____

_____   _____

_____   _____

Pure Trivia

Religious Holidays

Use your knowledge of religious holidays to name the special days described below.

1. A Muslim holy month of fasting, prayer, and devotion

_____

2. A Christian holiday commemorating the atonement, death, and resurrection of Jesus Christ

_____

3. A Jewish holiday celebrating the biblical liberation and exodus of the Israelites from captivity in Egypt

_____

4. A Hindu festival of lights

_____

5. A Jewish festival of lights, scripture, and singing, commemorating the rededication of the Holy Temple in Jerusalem

_____

Alphabet Soup

Solar System at a Glance

Using the hints below, unscramble the following list to determine the 8 planets in our solar system.

1. Largest planet, largest moon, and deepest oceans

PIUREJT

---

2. Most distant and slowest orbiting planet

PNNUEET

---

3. Moonless, smallest, and fastest orbiting planet

RYERUCM

---

4. Planet with the lowest average density and most moons

NAUSTR

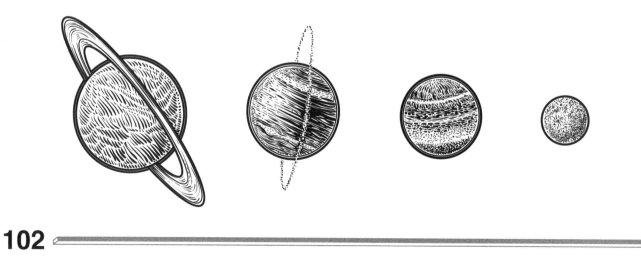

5. Planet with greatest average density and amount of liquid water on the surface

AREHT

6. Seventh planet that's icy and rotates on its side

SRUUAN

7. Hottest planet with the most circular orbit

UNVSE

8. Fourth planet and the tallest mountain; sometimes known as the red planet

RAMS

Alphabet Soup

Test Your Knowledge of the Equality State

Most people know Wyoming for its variety of plant and wildlife and its many beautiful national parks, natural monuments, and opportunities for recreation. Test how well you know Wyoming by unscrambling its various features and symbols below.

1. RTGAE LPNASI

_____

2. AKJNCSO LHEO

_____

3. YHECNEEN

_____

4. WSOYNETLOLE

_____

5. DGRNA TNETO

_____

Pure Trivia

Anatomy of a Cell

Match the cell parts in the word bank to the correct descriptions.

1. A double-stranded molecule with genetic information

_____

2. The center of a cell that contains most of the cell's genetic material

_____

3. Tiny components that lie outside the nucleus and supply chemical energy

_____

4. An outer covering that protects the cell

_____

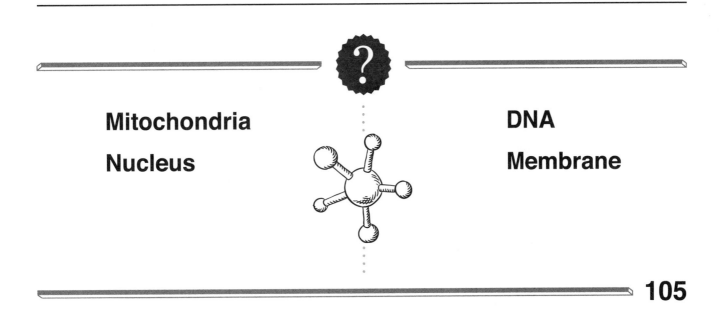

Mitochondria

Nucleus

DNA

Membrane

Alphabet Soup

Royal French Names

While the names of historical French royalty may not be as common today in the U.S. as their English counterparts, some of these French names have certainly come back into style in recent years. Some have fallen out of popularity, but you are sure to recognize them from history lessons. Test your recognition skills by unscrambling the five names below.

1. ISULO

_____

2. LIPHPI

_____

3. RALHCES

_____

4. CNARSIF

_____

5. NREYH

_____

Timed Test

Baseball's National League

Given 30 seconds, how many of the teams in Major League Baseball's National League can you list? Check the answer key to see whether you got all 15.

Pure Trivia

National Spelling Bee Words

Have you ever heard of these National Spelling Bee–winning words? Or their definitions? In classic pop-quiz fashion, select the correct answer for each of the definitions below.

1. A ribbed crepe fabric used in women's clothing
   a. Marocain
   b. Appoggiatura
   c. Guerdon
   d. Serrefine

2. A reward or recompense
   a. Prospicience
   b. Appoggiatura
   c. Guerdon
   d. Guetapens

3. A small forceps instrument used to clamp blood vessels
   a. Pococurante
   b. Cernuous
   c. Knaidel
   d. Serrefine

4. Foresight
   a. Serrefine
   b. Marocain
   c. Guetapens
   d. Prospicience

Alphabet Soup

Corporations That Begin With the Letter *C*

Using the hints about the services each corporation provides, unscramble the following list to see five of the most well-known corporations whose names begin with the letter *C*.

1. Food producer; parent company of V8, Pepperidge Farm, and Snyder's | LAPEBCML USPO

2. Soft drink producer | AOCC-LOAC

3. Television cable provider | MCSTOCA

4. Warehouse stores | TCSOOC LESAHELWO

5. Financial service provider that wonders "what's in your wallet?" | LATACIP NEO

Picture This

Famous Landmarks in the Eternal City

Use the answer bank to label the images of Rome landmarks.

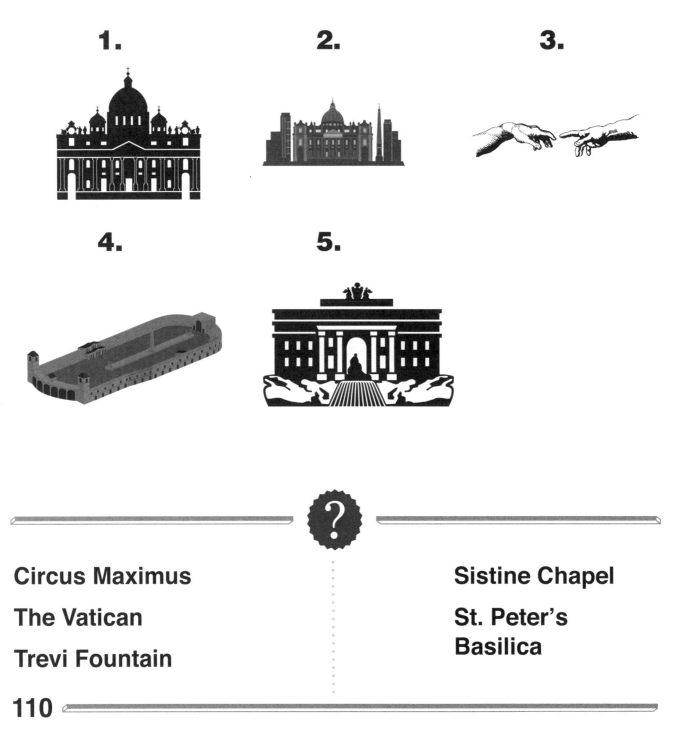

1.

2.

3.

4.

5.

?

Circus Maximus

The Vatican

Trevi Fountain

Sistine Chapel

St. Peter's Basilica

Pure Trivia

Puzzling Pseudonyms

For one reason or another, many entertainers choose to use a pseudonym or stage name. Most entertainers brand their stage names so well that the public never knows their real name. See if you can guess the true identities of some of these famous entertainers by matching the entertainer names with their less-famous counterparts.

1. ODYWO LNELA | Allan Konigsberg

2. NOBO | Paul Hewson

3. NAJO DROFRAWC | Lucille LeSueur

4. OBB YLNAD | Robert Zimmerman

5. UDJY RNALDAG | Frances Gumm

Alphabet Soup

Test Your Knowledge of the Pelican State

Most people know Louisiana for its fun celebrations, great food, and soulful music. Test how well you know Louisiana by unscrambling its various features and symbols below.

1. ZAJZ

_____

2. WNE RONESAL

_____

3. RAMDI ASRG

_____

4. OCLERE

_____

5. NHECFR RETAURQ

_____

Timed Test

Ruling Houses of England and the United Kingdom

Given 30 seconds, how many ruling houses of England and the UK can you list? We've given you two to get you started.

1. House of Stuart

2. The Saxons

Pure Trivia

Notable Writers of the Nineteenth Century

Each written work below is—arguably—among its author's most famous works. Can you fill in each author's name? Keep in mind that the author may have been born in the eighteenth century but had their writing debut during the nineteenth.

1. M _____ S _____
| *Frankenstein*

2. H _____ B _____
S _____ | *Uncle Tom's Cabin*

3. H _____ M _____
| *Moby Dick*

4. H _____ D _____
T _____ | "Civil Disobedience" and
Walden

5. M _____ T _____
| *The Adventures of Huckleberry Finn*

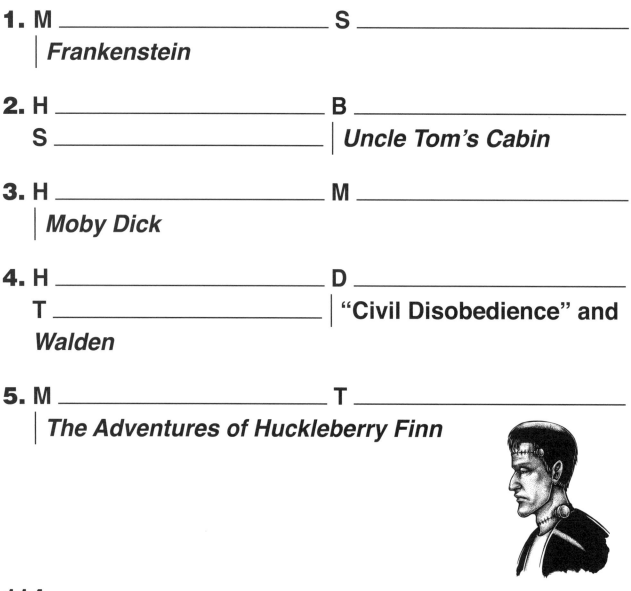

Picture This

Countries With the Largest Land Area

Use the answer bank to label the images of five countries with the largest land areas.

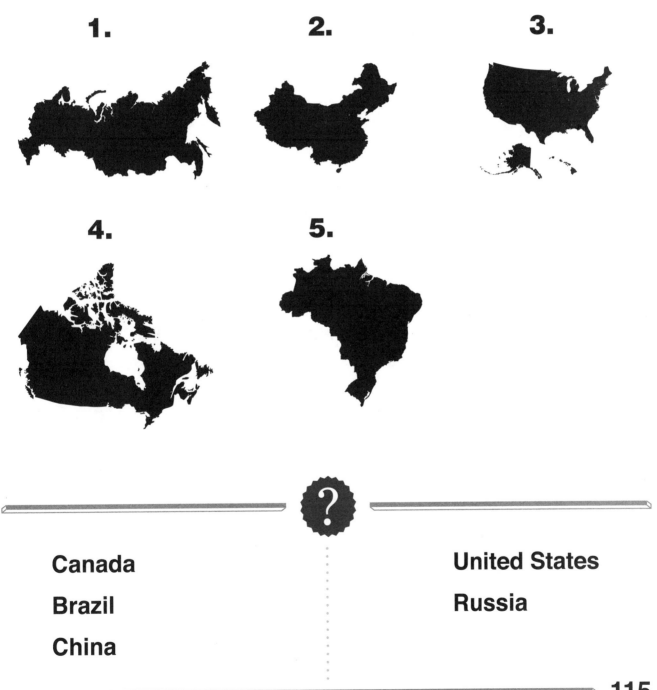

1.

2.

3.

4.

5.

?

Canada

Brazil

China

United States

Russia

Pure Trivia

Notable Scientists

The last few centuries have seen incredible progress in the fields of health and medicine, technology, and physics. Use the descriptions below to unscramble the accompanying names of scientists.

1. A physical chemist, pioneer investigator of radioactivity, and discoverer of radium and polonium
| IMAER UCREI

2. A naturalist who wrote *On the Origin of Species*
| LESRACH ARWIDN

3. A psychiatrist who pioneered psychoanalysis and wrote *Interpretation of Dreams* | DSNIUGM UFRDE

4. A physicist who explored gravity and black holes and wrote *A Brief History of Time* | ENSPTHE GINHWKA

5. A theoretical physicist known for his theory of relativity
| TALRBE NESINTEI

Picture This

Countries With the Largest Populations

Use the answer bank to label the images of five countries with the largest populations as of 2022.

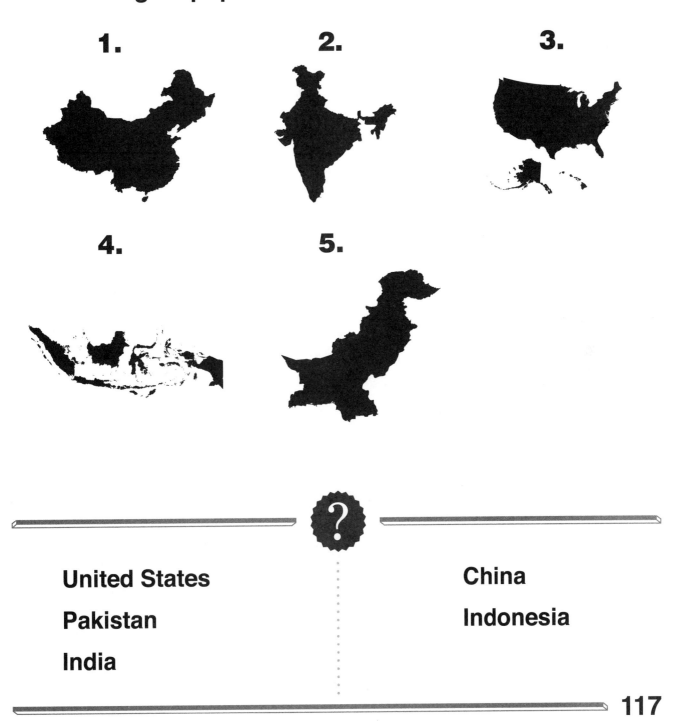

1.

2.

3.

4.

5.

?

United States

Pakistan

India

China

Indonesia

Timed Test

Football's American Football Conference (AFC)

Given 30 seconds, how many of the teams in the NFL's American Football Conference (AFC) can you list? Check the answer key to see whether you got all 16.

Alphabet Soup

Business Corporations That Begin With the Letter *D*

Using the hints about the services each corporation provides, unscramble the following list to see five of the most well-known corporations whose names begin with the letter *D.*

1. Computer and tech producer | LEDL

2. Airline company | ATELD

3. Satellite cable and media service | SIHD KNREOTW

4. Food products, fresh fruits, and vegetables producer | EDLO

5. News and stock corporation | WDO NSEJO

Picture This

Famous Landmarks in the District

Use the answer bank to label the images of landmarks in Washington, D.C.

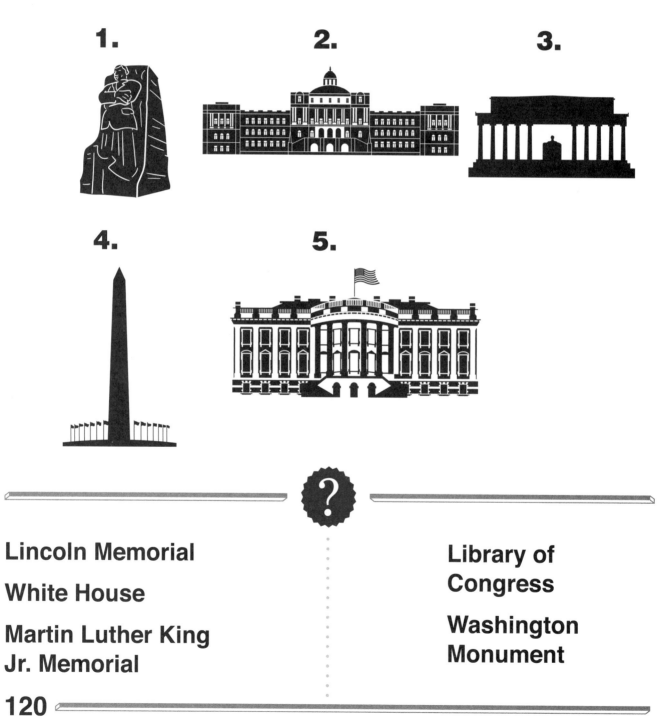

1.

2.

3.

4.

5.

Lincoln Memorial

White House

Martin Luther King
Jr. Memorial

Library of
Congress

Washington
Monument

Alphabet Soup

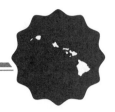

Test Your Knowledge of the Aloha State

Most people know Hawaii for its warm sands, clear beaches, and tropical plants and wildlife. Test how well you know Hawaii by unscrambling its various features and symbols below.

1. ANSILDS

_____

2. ULOHNLOU

_____

3. FRISUNG

_____

4. ISICBUSH

_____

5. SEVONACLO

_____

Timed Test

Largest U.S. Banks

Given 30 seconds, how many U.S. banking institutions can you list? Check your answers against the answer key for a list of some of the largest U.S. bank holding companies.

_____   _____

_____   _____

_____   _____

_____   _____

_____   _____

_____   _____

_____   _____

_____   _____

_____   _____

_____   _____

Picture This

Top U.S. Industries

Some countries excel in the oil industry, while others have achieved great success in tech and electronics. Which industries has the U.S. excelled in? Use the word bank to match the industry to its image.

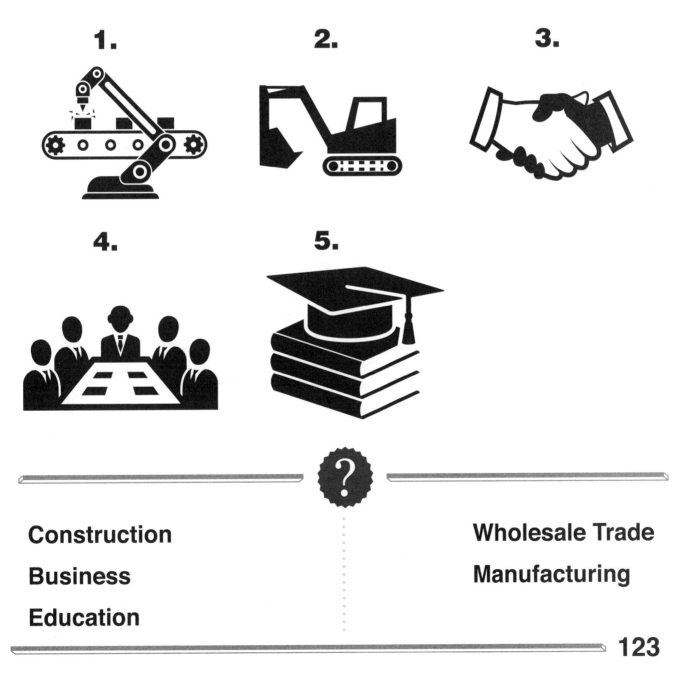

1.

2.

3.

4.

5.

Construction

Business

Education

Wholesale Trade

Manufacturing

Alphabet Soup

Notable Sports Personalities

Use the description clues to unscramble the names of some notable people in sports history.

1. Three-time heavyweight boxing champion, philanthropist, and social activist
| DAMHUMAM IAL

2. British soccer midfielder | DVADI CKMABHE

3. 23-time Grand Slam singles tennis champion and Olympic gold medalist | ASENRE LIASMLWI

4. Swimmer with the record for the most Olympic medals (28) and gold medals (23) held by a single athlete
| ALEHCMI SPHEPL

5. Track-and-field athlete who won 4 Olympic gold medals in 1936 | ESJSE ESNWO

Picture This

Famous Landmarks in the Big Apple

Use the answer bank to label the images of New York City landmarks.

1.

2.

3.

4.

5.

Brooklyn Bridge

Central Park

Metropolitan Museum of Art

Statue of Liberty

Empire State Building

Timed Test

Wealthy Educational Institutions

Many colleges and universities have endowment assets from generous donors. Given 30 seconds, how many schools can you name from the list of schools with the largest endowments? Hint: The schools that make up the Ivy League are among the top 26 highest endowed schools.

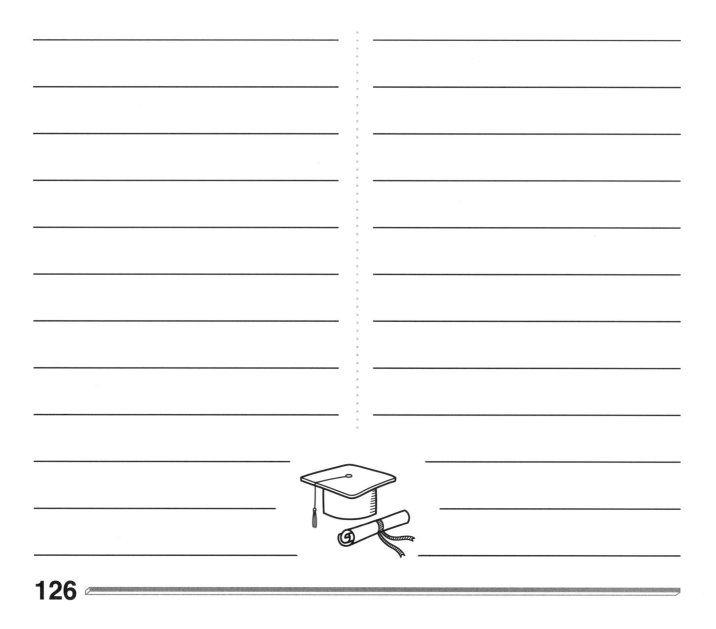

Picture This

U.S. Residents' Most Traveled-To Places

Does it surprise you to learn that, of all the U.S. citizens who traveled out of the country in 2019, only 6.6 percent of them traveled for business? That's right—a whopping 84.5 percent traveled out of the country for vacation or to visit friends or relatives. Which countries do you think they traveled to the most? Identify the countries below based on their images.

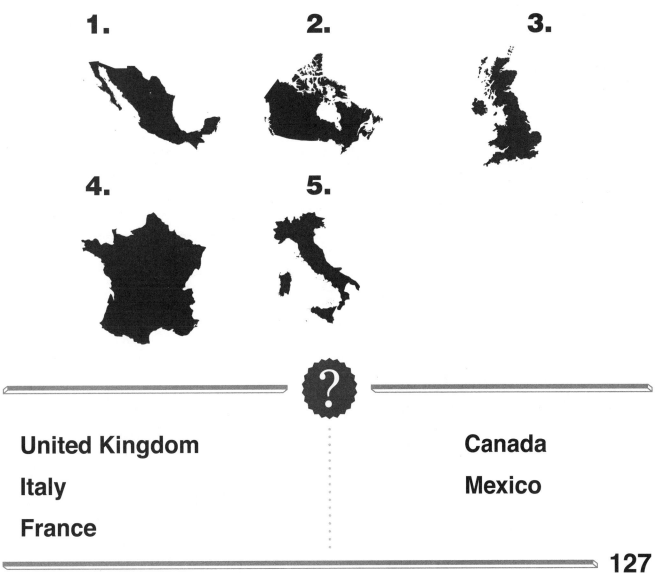

1.

2.

3.

4.

5.

United Kingdom

Italy

France

Canada

Mexico

Alphabet Soup

Basketball Legends

Use the description clues to unscramble the names of some of the greatest legends in basketball.

1. 4-time NBA MVP, and 4-time Finals MVP, with 4 NBA titles as of 2022 | NORLBE ASEJM

_____

2. Bulls star who won 6 NBA titles and was a 10-time leading NBA scorer and 5-time MVP | LMEIAHC DRAJNO

_____

3. Three-time NBA MVP and 3-time Finals MVP with 5 NBA titles with the Lakers | ACIGM ONJNSOH

_____

4. Lakers star who won 5 titles and was NBA MVP and NBA Finals MVP | BKEO TBAYNR

_____

5. Boston Celtics forward, NBA MVP, and coach of the year with Indiana Pacers | RALRY IDBR

_____

Pure Trivia

Top Brands

All of the following brands are top brands, but which ones beat out the rest? In classic pop-quiz fashion, select the top-selling brand in the U.S. for each of the products below.

1. Beer
   a. Coors Light
   b. Miller Lite
   c. Bud Light
   d. Michelob ULTRA

2. Bottled water
   a. Dasani
   b. Aquafina
   c. Nestlé Pure Life
   d. Poland Spring

3. Cereal
   a. Honey Bunches of Oats
   b. Cinnamon Toast Crunch
   c. Kellogg's Frosted Flakes
   d. Honey Nut Cheerios

4. Chocolate candy
   a. Lindt LINDOR
   b. M&M's
   c. Hershey's
   d. Reese's

5. Ground coffee
   a. Folgers
   b. Starbucks
   c. Maxwell House
   d. Dunkin' Donuts

Timed Test

Celebrated Renaissance Artists

Given 30 seconds, how many European Renaissance artists can you list?

_____

_____

_____

_____

_____

_____

_____

_____

_____

_____

_____

_____

_____

_____

_____

_____

_____

_____

_____

_____

Picture This

Visitors to the U.S.

The United States receives millions of visitors from around the world every year for purposes that range from business to vacation. Where do all these visitors come from? In addition to visitors from locations like Italy, France, Mexico, and the United Kingdom, the countries below are among the top ten in travelers to the U.S. Identify the countries below based on their images.

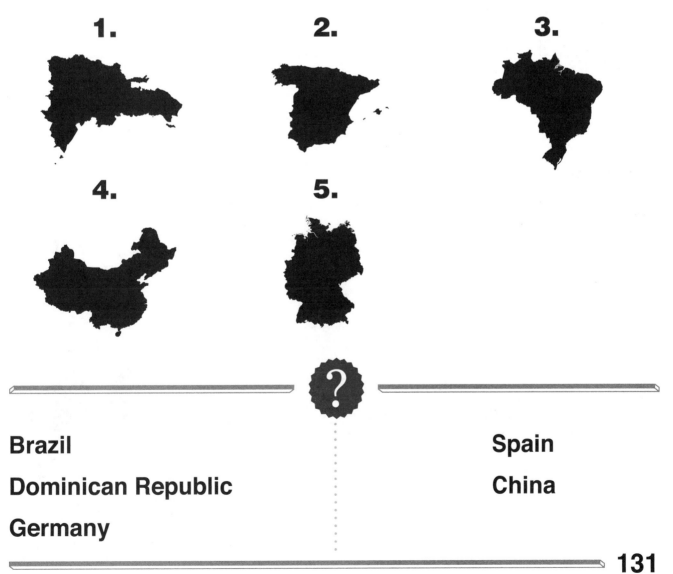

1.

2.

3.

4.

5.

Brazil

Dominican Republic

Germany

Spain

China

Alphabet Soup

Football Legends

Use the description clues to unscramble the names of some of the greatest legends in football.

1. Quarterback with 7 Super Bowl titles; a 5-time Super Bowl MVP and 3-time NFL MVP | MTO DYABR

2. Receiver with NFL record for career touchdowns (208) and receptions (1,549) | RYEJR IREC

3. NFL coach who led New England to 6 Super Bowl wins | LBIL ECKIHCBIL

4. Quarterback with a record 5 NFL MVP awards; a Super Bowl MVP; holds single-season passing yards record as of 2022 (5,477) | ONTPYE NGNIAMN

5. Won Super Bowls as coach of Oakland Raiders and was a longtime TV analyst; namesake for the popular NFL video game | NJHO DENMDA

Pure Trivia

Geology for Geniuses

In classic pop-quiz fashion, select the correct answer from each of the questions below.

1. Which type of rock is formed by the solidification of molten magma?
   a. igneous
   b. metamorphic
   c. sedimentary
   d. carbon fiber

2. Where is the Ring of Fire located?
   a. Caribbean Islands
   b. Indian Ocean
   c. Russia
   d. Pacific Rim

3. What is the name of the single supercontinent that scientists believe broke apart 200 million years ago to form the current continents?
   a. Gondwanaland
   b. Pangaea

   c. Jurassic Park
   d. Laurasia

4. Which of these rocks is a metamorphic rock?
   a. sandstone
   b. limestone
   c. obsidian
   d. marble

5. Which of these countries sits on a seam of tectonic plates?
   a. Russia
   b. Democratic Republic of the Congo
   c. Poland
   d. Switzerland

Picture This

Traveling Activities

Who doesn't love a good vacation? Vacation can mean different things to different people. Some vacationers set goals to see every notable landmark while other vacationers just want to do as little as necessary. A survey from the U.S. Department of Commerce tells us which leisure and recreational activities U.S. travelers prefer during their time out of the country. Use the answer bank to label the images of activities.

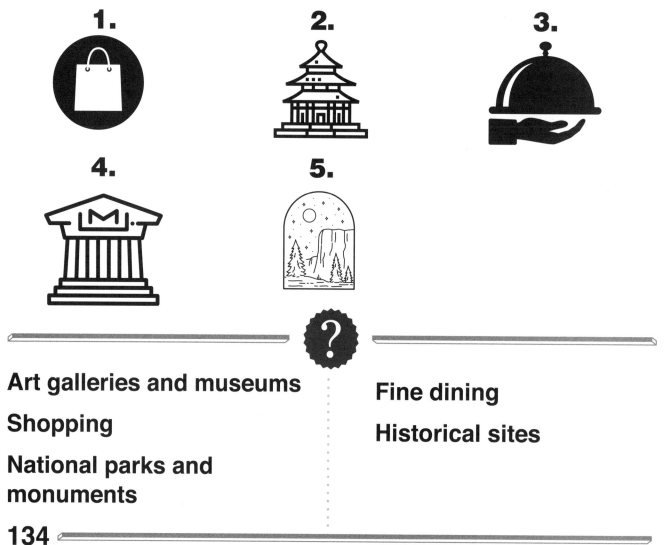

1.

2.

3.

4.

5.

Art galleries and museums

Shopping

National parks and monuments

Fine dining

Historical sites

Alphabet Soup

Baseball Legends

Use the description clues to unscramble the names of some of the greatest legends in baseball.

1. NY Yankees first baseman who played 2,130 straight games │ ULO GRHEGI

2. NY Yankees outfielder who hit 60 home runs during the 1927 season and 714 lifetime home runs; led the American League in home runs 12 times │ BEBA TUHR

3. Infielder who broke baseball's color barrier by joining the Brooklyn Dodgers in 1947 │ KECJAI NROBNISO

4. Giants center fielder who hit 660 home runs, had 3,283 hits, and was twice MVP │ LEIWIL ASYM

5. Shortstop who led NY Yankees to 5 World Series titles and was World Series MVP in 2000 │ EKDRE TERJE

Timed Test

Roman Rulers

Given 30 seconds, how many names of Roman rulers can you list?

Alphabet Soup

Corporations That Begin With the Letter *K*

Using the hints about the services each corporation provides, unscramble the following list to see four of the most well-known corporations whose names begin with the letter *K*.

1. Grocery and convenience store | GROKRE

_____

2. Food and beverage manufacturer | FTRKA HZNEI

_____

3. Cereal and other food product producer | SLGKOLEG

_____

4. Clothing, accessory, and décor designer | EKTA EPDSA

_____

Alphabet Soup

Advantageous U.S. Occupations

The U.S. Department of Labor put out a list of occupations that are projected to grow the most between the years 2020 and 2030. Test your recognition skills by unscrambling the occupations below to find out the top-five fastest-growing fields.

1. EMHO LAHTEH DEIA

_____

2. KOCO

_____

3. SFTA OFDO ORKWRE

_____

4. AREWFTSO EVLPROEDE

_____

5. DOFO VRESRE

_____

Timed Test

Countries Beginning With the Letter *C*

Given 30 seconds, how many countries beginning with the letter *C* can you name?

_____   _____

_____   _____

_____   _____

_____   _____

_____   _____

_____   _____

_____   _____

_____   _____

_____   _____

_____   _____

_____   _____

Alphabet Soup

Shrinking U.S. Occupations

The U.S. Department of Labor put out a list of occupations that are projected to decline the most between the years 2020 and 2030. Test your recognition skills by unscrambling the five occupations below to find out the top five jobs in decline.

1. SAHRIEC

_____

2. YRSETACRE NDA SANIATSTS

_____

3. TERLIA RVEISROUSP

_____

4. SBLESRAEM

_____

5. KBNA LETLER

_____

Pure Trivia

Science for Smarties

In classic pop-quiz fashion, select the correct answer from each of the questions below.

1. What is the periodic table symbol for the element iron?
- **a.** Cu
- **b.** I
- **c.** Fe
- **d.** N

2. How many elements are on the periodic table?
- **a.** 5
- **b.** 21
- **c.** 82
- **d.** 118

3. Which of the following is NOT a type of radiation?
- **a.** ultraviolet rays
- **b.** frost
- **c.** heat
- **d.** cosmic rays

4. What does the acronym "LED" stand for?
- **a.** luminous effects design
- **b.** light-emitting diode
- **c.** lingering-effects design
- **d.** light-enhancing device

Alphabet Soup

Corporations That Begin With the Letter *M*

Using the hints about the services each corporation provides, unscramble the following list to see five of the most well-known corporations whose names begin with the letter *M*.

1. Department store | SYMCA

2. Hotel franchise | RIORTAMT ALINONTETIRNA

3. Food manufacturer | SRMA

4. Financial services | DRACRESATM

5. Fast-food franchise | DCMONADLS

Timed Test

Countries Beginning With the Letter *L*

Given 30 seconds, how many countries beginning with the letter *L* can you name?

_____   _____

_____   _____

_____   _____

_____   _____

_____   _____

_____   _____

_____   _____

_____   _____

_____   _____

_____   _____

_____   _____

Pure Trivia

Greek Classics

How well do you know the key players and symbols of the Greek classics?

1. Who wrote the Greek epics *Iliad* and *Odyssey*?

2. Who are the three most cited philosophers of the fourth and fifth century BC?

3. What is the name of the piece of culminating architecture in Athens, built by Phidias?

4. Who was the drama writer known best for *Oedipus Rex*, *Antigone*, and *Ajax*?

5. In which city were the first national games observed, which celebrated male strength and beauty?

Alphabet Soup

Corporations That Begin With the Letter *N*

Using the hints about the services each corporation provides, unscramble the following list to see five of the most well-known corporations whose names begin with the letter *N*.

1. Upscale department store chain │ MORDSNTRO

2. Railway operator and freight carrier │ LKONFOR THSONRUE

3. Telecommunications equipment and computer software engineer │ KONAI

4. Athletic footwear and apparel corporation │ ENKI

5. Newspaper corporation │ WNE YKRO MTSIE

Timed Test

Countries Beginning With the Letter *M*

Given 30 seconds, how many countries beginning with the letter *M* can you name?

Alphabet Soup

Corporations That Begin With the Letter *S*

Using the hints about the services each corporation provides, unscramble the following list to see five of the most well-known corporations whose names begin with the letter *S*.

1. Homeowners' insurance provider │ ETSTA RFMA

2. World's leading specialty coffee retailer │ UCSTABKSR

3. Office-supply retailer │ SPLAETS

4. Hand and power tool manufacturer │ NATSEYL KACLB & ERCKED

5. Airline │ UOTHSTESW LINAIRES

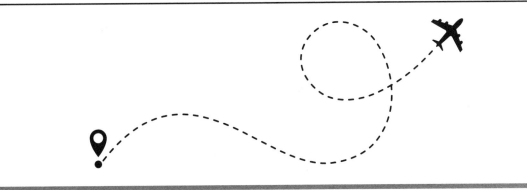

Pure Trivia

NBA Teams

Using the answer bank of NBA teams, match the teams with their hometowns.

1. Boston

_____

2. Phoenix

_____

3. Miami

_____

4. Chicago

_____

5. Los Angeles

_____

Heat

Clippers, Lakers

Bulls

Celtics

Suns

Timed Test

Countries Beginning With the Letter N

Given 30 seconds, how many countries beginning with the letter N can you name?

Alphabet Soup

Corporations That Begin With the Letter *W*

Using the hints about the services each corporation provides, unscramble the following list to see five of the most well-known corporations whose names begin with the letter *W*.

1. Motor home and recreational vehicle manufacturer
NEGOWBAIN

---

2. Major home appliance manufacturer | LPHIROWLO

---

3. Fast-food restaurant | NDEWYS'

---

4. Financial services provider and bank | SLELW RAFOG

---

5. Major media outlet | GTSNHIWANO STPO

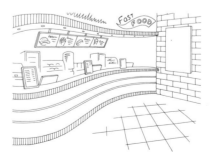

Timed Test

Countries Beginning With the Letter P

Given 30 seconds, how many countries beginning with the letter P can you name?

Timed Test

Football's National Football Conference (NFC)

Given 30 seconds, how many of the teams in the NFL's National Football Conference (NFC) can you list? Check the answer key to see whether you got all 16.

Pure Trivia

U.S. Presidents' First and Last Names

Match up each president's first name with their respective last name. Double points if you can include the party he was affiliated with (if any).

1. Theodore

_____

2. John

_____

3. Abraham

_____

4. George

_____

5. Barack

_____

Lincoln

Obama

Kennedy

Washington

Roosevelt

Timed Test

Countries Beginning With the Letter *T*

Given 30 seconds, how many countries beginning with the letter *T* can you name?

Pure Trivia

U.S. Capitals

Fill in the blanks next to the state capitals with their respective states.

1. Raleigh

_____

2. Montpelier

_____

3. Olympia

_____

4. Cheyenne

_____

5. Providence

_____

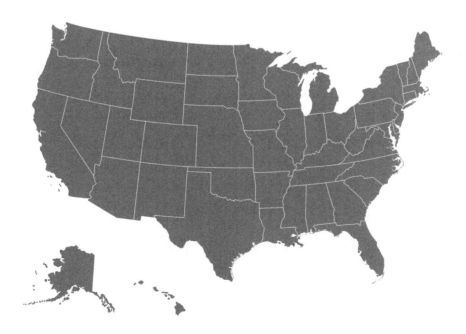

Pure Trivia

Rock & Roll Hall of Famers

Do you know which Rock & Roll Hall of Famers wrote these classic hits? Fill in the blank with the name of the band or artist.

1. "Don't Stop Believin'" _____

2. "Brown-Eyed Girl" _____

3. "Roxanne" _____

4. "Bohemian Rhapsody" _____

5. "My Girl" _____

Alphabet Soup

Who Owns What?

How well do you know the U.S. parent companies of these well-known consumer brands? Each of the brand groupings below has a parent company. Unscramble the accompanying names of the parent companies.

1. ABC Broadcasting and ESPN networks
TWLA YNESDI

2. American Girl, Fisher-Price, and Hot Wheels
TLETMA

3. Bounty, Cascade, Charmin, Cheer, Crest, Febreze, and Gillette | RORECTP & EGLABM

4. Betty Crocker, Pillsbury, and Yoplait | NERGELA SLIML

5. Grey Poupon, Jell-O, Kool-Aid, Maxwell House, Ore-Ida, and Oscar Mayer | TKFRA ZHNEI

Answer Key

Animal Collectives

Page 1

1. Cheetahs
2. Dolphins
3. Zebras
4. Jellyfish
5. Alligators
6. Flamingos
7. Owls
8. Otters
9. Hyenas
10. Finches

Do You Know Your U.S. National Parks?

Pages 2–3

1. Yellowstone, Idaho-Montana-Wyoming
2. Sequoia, California
3. Rocky Mountains, Colorado
4. Carlsbad Caverns, New Mexico
5. Everglades, Florida
6. Hot Springs, Arkansas
7. Crater Lake, Oregon
8. Acadia, Maine
9. Virgin Islands, Virgin Islands
10. Yosemite, California
11. Bryce Canyon, Utah

Countries Beginning With the Letter S

Page 4

Saint Kitts and Nevis

Saint Lucia

Saint Vincent and the Grenadines

Samoa

San Marino

São Tomé and Principe

Saudi Arabia

Senegal

Serbia

Seychelles

Sierra Leone

Singapore

Slovakia

Slovenia

Solomon Islands

Somalia

South Africa

South Korea

South Sudan

Spain

Sri Lanka

Sudan

Suriname

Sweden

Switzerland

Syria

Faces of U.S. Currency

Page 5

1. Quarter | George Washington

2. Nickel | Thomas Jefferson

3. $5 bill | Abraham Lincoln

4. $20 bill | Andrew Jackson

5. $100 bill | Benjamin Franklin

6. Half-dollar coin | John F. Kennedy

7. $1 coin | Sacagawea

Highest Rated Television Programs

Page 6

1. I Love Lucy

2. Bonanza

3. The Andy Griffith Show

4. Happy Days

5. Seinfeld

6. Friends

7. American Idol

2. Iron Man, Captain America, Thor, Hulk, Black Widow, and Hawkeye

3. Frodo, Sam, Merry, and Pippin

4. Bootstrap Bill

5. Heath Ledger

Popular Cat Breeds

Page 14

1. Persian

2. Ragdoll

3. Bengal

4. Sphynx

5. Maine Coon

U.S. National Monuments

Page 15

African Burial Ground

Agate Fossil Beds

Alibates Flint Quarries

Aniakchak

Aztec Ruins

Bandelier

Belmont-Paul Women's Equality

Birmingham Civil Rights

Booker T. Washington

Buck Island Reef

Cabrillo

Camp Nelson

Canyon de Chelly

Cape Krusenstern

Capulin Volcano

Casa Grande Ruins

Castillo de San Marcos

Castle Clinton

Castle Mountains

Cedar Breaks

César E. Chávez

Charles Young Buffalo Soldiers

Chiricahua

Colorado

Craters of the Moon

Devils Postpile

Devils Tower

Dinosaur

Effigy Mounds

El Malpais

El Morro

Florissant Fossil Beds

Fort Frederica

Fort Matanzas

Fort McHenry (and Historic Shrine)

Fort Monroe

Fort Pulaski

Fort Stanwix

Fort Union

Fossil Butte

Freedom Riders

George Washington Birthplace

George Washington Carver

Gila Cliff Dwellings

Governors Island

Grand Portage

Hagerman Fossil Beds

Hohokam Pima

Homestead NM of America

Hovenweep

Jewel Cave

John Day Fossil Beds

Katahdin Woods and Waters

Lava Beds

Little Bighorn Battlefield

Medgar and Myrlie Evers Home

Mill Springs Battlefield

Montezuma Castle

Muir Woods

Natural Bridges

Navajo

Oregon Caves (and Preserve)

Organ Pipe Cactus

Petroglyph

Pipe Spring

Pipestone

Poverty Point

Pullman

Rainbow Bridge

Russell Cave

Salinas Pueblo Missions

Scotts Bluff

Statue of Liberty

Stonewall

Sunset Crater Volcano

Timpanogos Cave

Tonto

Tule Lake

Tule Springs Fossil Beds

Tuzigoot

Virgin Islands Coral Reef

Waco Mammoth

Walnut Canyon

Wupatki

Yucca House

The Scientific Revolution

Page 16

1. Nicolaus Copernicus

2. Johannes Kepler

3. Galileo Galilei

4. Isaac Newton

Royal English Names

Page 17

1. William

2. Charles

3. James

4. Anne

5. Elizabeth

Notable Writers of the Twentieth Century

Page 18

1. Chinua Achebe

2. Maya Angelou

3. Eric Carle

4. Agatha Christie

5. Roald Dahl

Notable Ancient Greeks and Romans

Page 19

Aeschines, orator

Aeschylus, dramatist

Aesop, fableist

Alcibiades, politician

Ammianus, historian

Anacreon, poet

Anaxagoras, philosopher

Anaximander, philosopher

Anaximenes, philosopher

Antiphon, speechwriter

Antonius, politician

Apollonius, mathematician

Apuleius, satirist

Archimedes, mathematician

Aristophanes, dramatist

Aristotle, philosopher

Athenaeus, scholar

Augustus, politician

Top-Grossing Classic American Movies

Page 20

1. Jurassic Park
2. The Godfather
3. Gone with the Wind
4. Forrest Gump

Mongolia

Page 21

1. Singing Sands
2. Red Hero
3. Gobi Desert
4. Snow Leopard
5. Camel

Top Brands

Page 22

1. Lay's
2. Tostitos
3. Coca-Cola
4. Crest 3D White
5. Blue Bell

Visitors' Most Traveled-To Places in the U.S.

Page 23

1. California
2. Florida

3. New York

4. Texas

5. Georgia

Corporations That Begin With the Letter A

Pages 24–25

1. Apple

2. Amazon

3. American Express

4. Albertsons

5. Adidas

6. Allstate

7. Alaska Air

8. Alphabet

9. Aetna

10. Airbnb

Dietary Guidelines for Americans, 2020–2025

Page 26

Encouraged:

Vegetables

Fruits

Grains

Dairy (and Fortified Soy Alternatives)

Protein Foods

Oils

Limited:

Added Sugars

Saturated Fat

Sodium

Alcoholic Beverages

Most Crowded Countries

Page 27

1. Monaco

2. Singapore

3. Vatican City

4. Bahrain

5. Malta

Rock & Roll Hall of Famers

Page 28

1. AC/DC

2. Bon Jovi

3. Aerosmith

4. Fleetwood Mac

5. Eric Clapton

Religions of the World

Page 29

Agnosticism

Atheism

Baha'i

Buddhism

Catholicism

Confucianism

Hinduism

Independent Christian

Jainism

Judaism

Orthodox Christian

Protestantism

Shi'a Islam

Shinto

Sikhism

Spiritism

Sunni Islam

Taoism

Zoroastrianism

Animal Collectives

Page 30

1. Eagles

2. Hippopotamuses

3. Jellyfish

4. Larks

5. Kangaroos

6. Bears

7. Buffalo

8. Cranes

9. Foxes

10. Nightingales

Common Acronyms

Page 31

1. Absent Without Leave

2. Be Right Back

3. Self-Contained Underwater Breathing Apparatus

4. Most Valuable Player

5. Science, Technology, Engineering, Math

U.S. Constitution

Page 32

1. People
2. Union
3. Justice
4. domestic
5. defence
6. Welfare
7. Liberty
8. Posterity
9. Establish
10. Constitution

Classical Composers

Page 33

1. J.S. Bach
2. Beethoven
3. Vivaldi
4. Tchaikovsky
5. Mozart

Olympic Winter Sports

Page 34

1. Curling
2. Figure Skating
3. Ice Hockey
4. Snowboarding
5. Ski Jumping

U.S. Medals of Honor

Page 35

1. Medal of Honor
2. Soldier's Medal
3. Silver Star
4. Air Medal

Top Sources of Sugar in U.S. Diets

Page 36

1. Beverages
2. Desserts
3. Breakfast cereals
4. Candy

Award-Winning Children's Books

Page 37

1. Island of the Blue Dolphins (Scott O'Dell)

2. A Wrinkle in Time (Madeleine L'Engle)

3. Bud, Not Buddy (Christopher Paul Curtis)

4. Roll of Thunder, Hear My Cry (Mildred D. Taylor)

Components of Nutrition

Page 38

1. Vitamin A

2. Calcium builds and maintains bones and teeth.

3. Leafy vegetables

4. Proteins

Countries Beginning With the Letter *A*

Page 39

Afghanistan

Albania

Algeria

Andorra

Angola

Antigua and Barbuda

Argentina

Armenia

Australia

Austria

Azerbaijan

Notable Writers of the Twentieth Century

Page 40

1. F. Scott Fitzgerald

2. Robert Frost

3. William Golding

4. Ernest Hemingway

5. James Joyce

World's Wealthiest Individuals

Page 41

1. Jeff Bezos

2. Bill Gates

3. Warren Buffett

4. Mark Zuckerberg

5. Larry Page

Things U.S. States Are Notable For

Pages 42–43

1. Georgia
2. Utah
3. Oregon
4. Minnesota
5. Louisiana
6. Tennessee
7. Wisconsin
8. New York
9. Alaska
10. Rhode Island

Top Motor Vehicle–Producing Nations

Page 44

1. China
2. U.S.
3. Japan
4. Germany
5. India

Rock & Roll Hall of Famers

Page 45

1. Lynyrd Skynyrd
2. Billy Joel
3. Stevie Nicks
4. The Beatles
5. Led Zeppelin

Edison's Inventions

Page 46

1. Kinetoscope
2. Phonograph
3. Wax cylinder record
4. Quadruplex telegraph

Innovation in Technology

Page 47

1. 1447: Gutenberg brings movable type to Europe
2. 1866: The first successful transatlantic telegraph cable is laid

3. 1903: The Wright Brothers invent the first motor-powered airplane

4. 1994: Invention of the first smartphone

5. 2007: Apple releases the first iPhone

Test Your Knowledge of the Last Frontier

Page 48

1. Northern Lights

2. Fishing

3. Midnight Sun

4. Juneau

5. Dog Mushing

U.S. Capitals

Page 49

1. Springfield, Illinois

2. Sacramento, California

3. Tallahassee, Florida

4. Boise, Idaho

5. Bismarck, North Dakota

Award-Winning Children's Books

Page 50

1. Maniac Magee | Jerry Spinelli

2. Holes | Louis Sachar

3. The Giver | Lois Lowry

4. Walk Two Moons | Sharon Creech

5. The Tale of Despereaux | Kate DiCamillo

Baby Animals

Page 51

1. Sheep | Lamb

2. Swan | Cygnet

3. Goose | Gosling

4. Hedgehog | Hoglet

5. Kangaroo | Joey

Notable Writers of the Twentieth Century

Page 52

1. George Orwell

2. J. D. Salinger

3. Dr. Seuss

Burma (Myanmar)

Burundi

U.S. Capitals

Page 57

1. Hartford, Connecticut
2. Augusta, Maine
3. Boston, Massachusetts
4. Jackson, Mississippi
5. Helena, Montana

Timeline of Architectural Styles

Page 58

1. Egyptian
2. Roman
3. Renaissance
4. Art Deco
5. Postmodernism

U.S. Declaration of Independence

Page 59

1. Truths
2. evident

3. Men
4. equal
5. Creator
6. Rights
7. Life
8. Liberty
9. Pursuit
10. Happiness

Grammy Awards

Page 60

1. Henry Mancini
2. Simon and Garfunkel
3. The Eagles
4. Billy Joel
5. Carole King

Life Cycles of Animals

Page 61

1. Gorilla, 5
2. Giraffe, 4
3. Opossum, 1
4. Mouse, 2
5. Wolf, 3

Olympic Summer Sports

Page 62

1. Gymnastics
2. Swimming & Diving
3. Tennis
4. Track & Field
5. Volleyball

Academy Awards (Oscars) for Best Picture

Page 63

A. Gone with the Wind

B. Humphrey Bogart

C. Audrey Hepburn

D. Julie Andrews

E. Jack Nicholson

F. The Godfather

G. Rain Man

H. Jodie Foster

I. Liam Neeson

J. Braveheart

English's Borrowed Words and Phrases

Pages 64–65

1. ad hoc | Latin | impromptu; for the end or purpose at hand

2. chutzpah | Yiddish | audacity or nerve

3. doppelgänger | German | a double or counterpart of a person

4. deus ex machina | Latin | a person or event that provides an unexpected, often miraculous and contrived, solution to a problem

5. je ne sais quoi | French | "I don't know what"; the little something that eludes description

6. ombudsman | Swedish | a person who receives, investigates, and settles complaints

7. pariah | Tamil | an outcast; a member of a lower class or caste

Grenada

Guatemala

Guinea

Guinea-Bissau

Guyana

Mohs Scale of Hardness

Page 71

1. Talc

2. Gypsum

3. Calcite

4. Fluorite

5. Apatite

6. Feldspar

7. Quartz

8. Topaz

9. Corundum

10. Diamond

Top Sources of Saturated Fat in U.S. Diets

Page 72

1. sandwiches

2. desserts

3. rice/pasta dishes

4. milk

5. pizza

Most Populated U.S. Cities

Page 73

1. New York

2. California

3. Illinois

4. Pennsylvania

5. Texas

Notable Writers of the Nineteenth Century

Page 74

1. Alexandre Dumas

2. Ralph Waldo Emerson

3. Nathaniel Hawthorne

4. Victor Hugo

5. John Keats

The Bill of Rights—10 Amendments

Page 75

1. Amendment 8
2. Amendment 1
3. Amendment 2
4. Amendment 6
5. Amendment 10
6. Amendment 9
7. Amendment 4
8. Amendment 3
9. Amendment 5
10. Amendment 7

Test Your Knowledge of the Lone Star State

Page 76

1. Alamo
2. River Walk
3. Bluebonnet
4. Panhandle
5. Sam Houston

Modern History: 1997

Page 77

1. Mars Pathfinder
2. Diana, Princess of Wales
3. Titanic
4. Harry Potter
5. "My Heart Will Go On"

Great Impressionists

Page 78

Jean Frédéric Bazille

Marie Bracquemond

Gustave Caillebotte

Mary Cassatt

Paul Cézanne

Edgar Degas

Eva Gonzalès

Childe Hassam

Édouard Manet

Henri Matisse

Claude Monet

Berthe Morisot

2. Galileo

3. Magellan

4. Voyager 2

Venomous Animals

Page 85

ants, bees, hornets, wasps

Asian cobra

Asian pit viper

Australian black snake

Australian brown snake

barba amarilla

black mamba

black widow

boomslang

brown recluse

Bruno's casque-headed frog

Bushmaster

catfish (some species)

chimaera

cockatoo waspfish

cone-shell

copperhead

coral snake

cottonmouth water moccasin

death adder

desert horned viper

dogfish

Eurasian water shrew

European viper

fire salamander

funnel web spider

Gaboon viper

Gila monster

goblinfish

Greening's frog

king cobra

krait

lancehead viper

lionfish

man-of-war jellyfish

Mexican beaded lizard

Octopus

platypus

puff adder

rabbitfish

rattlesnake

ringhals/spitting viper

Russell's viper

scorpion

scorpionfish

sea snake

sea wasp/box jellyfish

sharp-nosed pit viper

short-tailed shrew
(northern and southern)

solenodon

soral snake

stargazer fish

stingray

stonefish

striped blenny

taipan

tarantula

tiger snake

toadfish

weeverfish

yellow/cape cobra

World's Speediest Species

Page 86

1. Cheetah

2. Pronghorn Antelope

3. Wildebeest

4. Lion

5. Gazelle

Corporations That Begin With the Letter *B*

Page 87

1. Barnes & Noble

2. Berkshire Hathaway

3. Best Buy

4. Boeing

5. Bank of America

Animal Collectives

Page 88

1. Ducks

2. Locusts

3. Leopards

Pleistocene Epoch

Pliocene Epoch

Proterozoic Eon

Quaternary Period

Silurian Period

Triassic Period

Modern History: 1972

Page 92

1. Bloody Sunday
2. Equal Rights Amendment
3. Watergate
4. Apollo 17

Tony Award–Winning Musicals

Page 93

1. Les Misérables
2. Phantom of the Opera
3. The Sound of Music
4. Fiddler on the Roof
5. Cats

Baby Animals

Page 94

1. Kid
2. Tadpole
3. Pup
4. Squab
5. Ephyra

Royal Scottish Names

Page 95

1. Robert
2. James
3. Alexander
4. Mary
5. Margaret

Baseball's American League

Page 96

1. Baltimore Orioles
2. Boston Red Sox
3. Chicago White Sox
4. Cleveland Guardians
5. Detroit Tigers

6. Houston Astros

7. Kansas City Royals

8. Los Angeles Angels

9. Minnesota Twins

10. New York Yankees

11. Oakland Athletics

12. Seattle Mariners

13. Tampa Bay Rays

14. Texas Rangers

15. Toronto Blue Jays

Top-Selling Light Trucks in the U.S.

Page 97

1. Ford F-Series

2. Ram Pickup

3. Chevrolet Silverado

4. Toyota RAV4

5. Honda CR-V

Best-in-Show Dog Breeds

Page 98

1. Poodle

2. Fox Terrier

3. German Shepherd

4. Beagle

5. Pug

Countries With Deserts

Page 99

1. United States

2. Sudan

3. Argentina

4. Australia

5. Egypt

Country Capitals Beginning With the Letter *B*

Page 100

Baghdad

Baku

Bamako

Bandar Seri Begawan

Bangkok

Bangui

Banjul

Basseterre

Beijing

Beirut

Belfast

Belgrade

Belmopan

Berlin

Bern

Bishkek

Bissau

Bogota

Brasilia

Bratislava

Brazzaville

Bridgetown

Brussels

Bucharest

Budapest

Buenos Aires

Religious Holidays

Page 101

1. Ramadan

2. Easter Sunday

3. Passover

4. Diwali

5. Hanukkah

Solar System at a Glance

Pages 102–103

1. Jupiter

2. Neptune

3. Mercury

4. Saturn

5. Earth

6. Uranus

7. Venus

8. Mars

Test Your Knowledge of the Equality State

Page 104

1. Great Plains

2. Jackson Hole

3. Cheyenne

4. Yellowstone

5. Grand Teton

Anatomy of a Cell

Page 105

1. DNA
2. Nucleus
3. Mitochondria
4. Membrane

Royal French Names

Page 106

1. Louis
2. Philip
3. Charles
4. Francis
5. Henry

Baseball's National League

Page 107

1. Arizona Diamondbacks
2. Atlanta Braves
3. Chicago Cubs
4. Cincinnati Reds
5. Colorado Rockies
6. Los Angeles Dodgers
7. Miami Marlins
8. Milwaukee Brewers
9. New York Mets
10. Philadelphia Phillies
11. Pittsburgh Pirates
12. St. Louis Cardinals
13. San Diego Padres
14. San Francisco Giants
15. Washington Nationals

National Spelling Bee Words

Page 108

1. Marocain
2. Guerdon
3. Serrefine
4. Prospicience

Corporations That Begin With the Letter *C*

Page 109

1. Campbell Soup
2. Coca-Cola
3. Comcast

4. Costco Wholesale

5. Capital One

Famous Landmarks in the Eternal City

Page 110

1. St. Peter's Basilica

2. The Vatican

3. Sistine Chapel

4. Circus Maximus

5. Trevi Fountain

Puzzling Pseudonyms

Page 111

1. Woody Allen

2. Bono

3. Joan Crawford

4. Bob Dylan

5. Judy Garland

Test Your Knowledge of the Pelican State

Page 112

1. Jazz

2. New Orleans

3. Mardi Gras

4. Creole

5. French Quarter

Ruling Houses of England and the United Kingdom

Page 113

The Saxons

The Danes

House of Normandy

House of Blois

House of Plantagenet

House of Lancaster

House of York

House of Tudor

House of Stuart

House of Hanover

House of Saxe-Coburg-Gotha

House of Windsor

Notable Writers of the Nineteenth Century

Page 114

1. Mary Shelley
2. Harriet Beecher Stowe
3. Herman Melville
4. Henry David Thoreau
5. Mark Twain

Countries With the Largest Land Area

Page 115

1. Russia
2. China
3. United States
4. Canada
5. Brazil

Notable Scientists

Page 116

1. Marie Curie
2. Charles Darwin
3. Sigmund Freud
4. Stephen Hawking
5. Albert Einstein

Countries With the Largest Populations

Page 117

1. China
2. India
3. United States
4. Indonesia
5. Pakistan

Football's American Football Conference (AFC)

Page 118

1. Baltimore Ravens
2. Buffalo Bills
3. Cincinnati Bengals
4. Cleveland Browns
5. Denver Broncos
6. Houston Texans
7. Indianapolis Colts
8. Jacksonville Jaguars
9. Kansas City Chiefs
10. Las Vegas Raiders

11. Los Angeles Chargers

12. Miami Dolphins

13. New England Patriots

14. New York Jets

15. Pittsburgh Steelers

16. Tennessee Titans

Corporations That Begin With the Letter *D*

Page 119

1. Dell

2. Delta

3. Dish Network

4. Dole

5. Dow Jones

Famous Landmarks in the District

Page 120

1. Martin Luther King Jr. Memorial

2. Library of Congress

3. Lincoln Memorial

4. Washington Monument

5. White House

Test Your Knowledge of the Aloha State

Page 121

1. Islands

2. Honolulu

3. Surfing

4. Hibiscus

5. Volcanoes

Largest U.S. Banks

Page 122

Ally Financial

American Express

Ameriprise

Bank of America

Bank of New York Mellon

Barclays

Capital One

Charles Schwab

Citigroup

Citizens

Discover

Goldman Sachs

HSBC Bank

JPMorgan Chase

KeyCorp

M & T Bank

Morgan Stanley

Northern Trust

PNC Financial Services

RBC Bank

Santander

SVB

Synchrony

TD Bank

Truist

USAA

U.S. Bancorp

Wells Fargo

Top U.S. Industries
Page 123
1. Manufacturing
2. Construction
3. Wholesale Trade
4. Business

5. Education

Notable Sports Personalities

Page 124
1. Muhammad Ali
2. David Beckham
3. Serena Williams
4. Michael Phelps
5. Jesse Owens

Famous Landmarks in the Big Apple

Page 125
1. Central Park
2. Statue of Liberty
3. Empire State Building
4. Brooklyn Bridge
5. Metropolitan Museum of Art

Wealthy Educational Institutions

Page 126
Amherst College

Boston College

Brown University

California Institute of Technology

Carnegie Mellon University

Columbia University

Cornell University

Dartmouth College

Duke University

Emory University

Harvard University

Johns Hopkins University

Massachusetts Institute of Technology

Michigan State University

New York University

Northwestern University

Ohio State University

Pennsylvania State University

Princeton University

Purdue University

Rice University

Stanford University

Texas A&M University System

UCLA

University of California

University of Chicago

University of Michigan

University of Minnesota

University of North Carolina at Chapel Hill

University of Notre Dame

University of Pennsylvania

University of Pittsburgh

University of Southern California

University of Texas System

University of Virginia

University of Washington

University of Wisconsin

Vanderbilt University

Washington University

Williams College

Yale University

U.S. Residents' Most Traveled-To Places

Page 127

1. Mexico
2. Canada
3. United Kingdom
4. France
5. Italy

Basketball Legends

Page 128

1. LeBron James
2. Michael Jordan
3. "Magic" Johnson
4. Kobe Bryant
5. Larry Bird

Top Brands

Page 129

1. Bud Light
2. Aquafina
3. Honey Nut Cheerios
4. M&M's
5. Folgers

Celebrated Renaissance Artists

Page 130

Fra Angelico

Gentile Bellini

Giovanni Bellini

Jacop Bellini

Hieronymus Bosch

Sandro Botticelli

Pieter Bruegel the Elder

Antonio da Correggio

Luca della Robbia

Donatello

Albrecht Dürer

Lorenzo Ghiberti

Giorgione

Giotto di Bondone

El Greco

Hans Holbein the Elder

Hans Holbein the Younger

Leonardo da Vinci

Filippino Lippi

Fra Filippo Lippi

Andrea Mantegna

Masaccio

Michelangelo di Lodovico Buonarroti Simoni

Pietro Perugino

Piero della Francesca

Raphael Sanzio da Urbino

Andrea Sansovino

Jacopo Sansovino

Titian

Paolo Ucello

Visitors to the U.S.

Page 131

1. Dominican Republic

2. Spain

3. Brazil

4. China

5. Germany

Football Legends

Page 132

1. Tom Brady

2. Jerry Rice

3. Bill Belichick

4. Peyton Manning

5. John Madden

Geology for Geniuses

Page 133

1. igneous

2. Pacific Rim

3. Pangaea

4. marble

5. Russia

Traveling Activities

Page 134

1. Shopping

2. Historical sites

3. Fine dining

4. Art galleries and museums

5. National parks and monuments

Baseball Legends

Page 135

1. Lou Gehrig

2. Babe Ruth

3. Jackie Robinson

4. Willie Mays

5. Derek Jeter

Roman Rulers

Page 136

Alexander

Anthemius

Antoninus

Arcadius

Augustus

Aurelian

Avitus

Caligula

Carinus

Carus

Claudius

Commodus

Constantine

Constantius

Didius

Diocletian

Domitian

Eugenius

Florian

Galba

Galerius

Gallienus

Gallus

Glycerius

Gordian

Gratian

Hadrian

Honorius

Jovian

Julian

Julius

Leo

Libius

Magnus

Majorian

Marcian

Marcus

Maximus

Nero

Nerva

Octavian

Otho

Petronius

Philip

Probus

Quintillus

Romulus

Severus

Tacitus

Theodosius

Tiberius

Titus

Trajan

Valens

Valerian

Vanentinian

Corporations That Begin With the Letter K

Page 137

1. Kroger

2. Kraft Heinz

3. Kellogg's

4. Kate Spade

Advantageous U.S. Occupations

Page 138

1. Home Health Aide

2. Cook

3. Fast Food Worker

4. Software Developer

5. Food Server

Countries Beginning With the Letter C

Page 139

Cabo Verde

Cambodia

Cameroon

Canada

Central African Republic

Chad

Chile

China

Colombia

Comoros

Congo, Democratic Republic of the

Congo Republic

Costa Rica

Côte d'Ivoire

Croatia

Cuba

Cyprus

Czechia

Shrinking U.S. Occupations

Page 140

1. Cashier

2. Secretary and Assistant

3. Retail Supervisor

4. Assembler

5. Bank Teller

Science for Smarties

Page 141

1. Fe

2. 118

3. frost

4. light-emitting diode

Corporations That Begin With the Letter *M*

Page 142

1. Macy's

2. Marriott International

3. Mars

4. MasterCard

5. McDonald's

Countries Beginning With the Letter *L*

Page 143

Laos

Latvia

Lebanon

Lesotho

Liberia

Libya

Liechtenstein

Lithuania

Luxembourg

Greek Classics

Page 144

1. Homer
2. Aristotle, Socrates, Plato
3. Parthenon
4. Sophocles
5. Olympia

Corporations That Begin With the Letter *N*

Page 145

1. Nordstrom
2. Norfolk Southern
3. Nokia
4. Nike
5. New York Times

Countries Beginning With the Letter M

Page 146

Madagascar

Malawi

Malaysia

Maldives

Mali

Malta

Marshall Islands

Mauritania

Mauritius

Mexico

Micronesia

Moldova

Monaco

Mongolia

Montenegro

Morocco

Mozambique

Myanmar

Corporations That Begin With the Letter *S*

Page 147

1. State Farm
2. Starbucks
3. Staples
4. Stanley Black & Decker
5. Southwest Airlines

NBA Teams

Page 148

1. Boston Celtics
2. Phoenix Suns
3. Miami Heat
4. Chicago Bulls
5. Los Angeles Clippers, Los Angeles Lakers

Countries Beginning With the Letter N

Page 149

Namibia

Nauru

Nepal

Netherlands

New Zealand

Nicaragua

Niger

Nigeria

North Korea

North Macedonia

Norway

Corporations That Begin With the Letter W

Page 150

1. Winnebago
2. Whirlpool
3. Wendy's
4. Wells Fargo
5. Washington Post

Countries Beginning With the Letter P

Page 151

Pakistan

Palau

Palestine

Panama

Papua New Guinea

Paraguay

Peru

Philippines

Poland

Portugal

Football's National Football Conference (NFC)

Page 152

1. Arizona Cardinals
2. Atlanta Falcons
3. Carolina Panthers
4. Chicago Bears
5. Dallas Cowboys
6. Detroit Lions
7. Green Bay Packers
8. Los Angeles Rams
9. Minnesota Vikings
10. New Orleans Saints
11. New York Giants
12. Philadelphia Eagles
13. San Francisco 49ers
14. Seattle Seahawks
15. Tampa Bay Buccaneers
16. Washington Commanders

U.S. Presidents' First and Last Names

Page 153

Theodore Roosevelt | Republican

John F. Kennedy | Democrat

Abraham Lincoln | Republican or National Union

George Washington | unaffiliated

Barack Obama | Democrat

Countries Beginning With the Letter *T*

Page 154

Tajikistan

Tanzania

Thailand

Timor-Leste

Togo

Tonga

Trinidad and Tobago

Tunisia

Turkey (or Türkiye)

Turkmenistan

Tuvalu

U.S. Capitals

Page 155

1. Raleigh, North Carolina

2. Montpelier, Vermont

3. Olympia, Washington

4. Cheyenne, Wyoming

5. Providence, Rhode Island

Rock & Roll Hall of Famers

Page 156

1. Journey

2. Van Morrison

3. The Police

4. Queen

5. The Temptations

Who Owns What?

Page 157

1. Walt Disney

2. Mattel

3. Procter & Gamble

4. General Mills

5. Kraft Heinz